*Letters to Strongheart*

STRONGHEART

*Photo by Paul Grenbeaux*

# LETTERS TO *Strongheart*

*by*

## J. ALLEN BOONE

Robert H. Sommer, Publisher
Harrington Park, New Jersey 07640
1977

ISBN-978-0-933062-19-1
Printed In United States of America

## TO THE READER

If you are one of the many millions who came to know and love Strongheart through the medium of motion pictures, you can perhaps understand how anyone might like to write letters to him. As a matter of fact, so many of you did that that the volume of his mail, when he was at the height of his career as a film celebrity, was a constant surprise to the officials of the Hollywood post office. Perhaps you still cherish one of his photographs with his autograph in one of the lower corners. He liked autographing things. He did it by placing one of his front feet on a special ink-pad and then pressing it down on whatever needed the signature.

Transforming a prize-winning, police-trained German shepherd dog into a movie star, building dramatic plays around him, and providing a cast of human actors to support him was a novel idea at the time. And a very successful one too. The first film created such widespread interest and enthusiasm that Strongheart became an overnight sensation. Within a few months his fame had become international. Thereafter, each succeeding picture added to his reputation and deepened the affection men, women, and children all over the world had for him. Much of this, no doubt, was due to the fact that few people had ever before seen a dog of his type, size, intelligence, and accomplishments in action, plus the oddity of a dog as the " leading man " in movie dramas.

One day when his success was at its peak, word was flashed from Hollywood that Strongheart was dead. A sudden illness, and then the end. The entire world was shocked and saddened. To his many admirers, it was a personal loss. To the picture industry, it meant the loss of its most unique performer, and one of its best box-office attractions. As time moved along in its swift pace and with its kaleidoscopic changes, people began dropping Strongheart from their thinking areas, except as a memory of a dog that had been thrilling to watch but was now dead. I could not do this, though. Strongheart happens to be my pal. He was my pal. He still is my pal. Circumstances sent him into my individual mental world of awareness, and as long as he got in there and added so much to it, I shall take precious good care that nothing shoves him out again. And I can do that, because I happen to be the one who thinks about the things that go on in my individual world of awareness.

As a citizen of the Cosmos, I refuse to give my consent to the popular belief that any friend of mine, whether classified as a human or an animal, is "dead and gone forever" simply because my limited, faulty, material senses are unable to identify him in their immediate vicinity. I have learned to look at life with something more real than material senses. And that " something," let me add, concedes no reality whatsoever to the phenomenon of death. I mention this because as you turn the next few pages you will come upon letters that I have written to what the world regards as " a dead dog "; and since writing letters to " dead dogs " is not orthodox procedure among the human species, you are entitled to some sort of explanation. The letters must speak for themselves. But as you read them, may I remind you that they were written to Strongheart? That automatically puts you in the position of having to read them over his shoulder, so to speak. I do hope it will be an interesting experience for you.

Now about Strongheart. As you probably remember, he shot through the entertainment world like a luminous meteor. First came " The Silent Call." Then, " Brawn of the North." Then, " The Love Master." Then, " White Fang." Before his appearance in pictures, the German shepherd dog with police training was little known in the United States. But he more than made up for it after his dramatic arrival. He not only popularized his breed in this country, but stimulated an unprecedented interest in dogs throughout the world.

The two people responsible for his success were Jane Murfin, the distinguished writer of stage and screen plays, and Larry Trimble, a motion-picture director with unusual gifts for persuading wild and domestic animals to perform at their best in front of cameras. Trimble was Strongheart's tutor and director. My relationships with the dog were entirely those of a friend. For quite a period of time we lived together—kept house together, as a matter of fact. I had nothing to do with his education or the making of his pictures. When I first met him, he was so well-educated and knew so much more than I did about so many important things in the universe that I had to let him teach me in order to keep intelligent company with him. He was an amazing dog in public performance, but he was even more so as a friend in private life.

Strongheart's kennel name was Etzel von Oeringen. He was born in Germany, the son of Nores von der Kriminal Politzei, an undefeated champion for some time. The only dog ever capable of topping him in show and field trials was his own son, Etzel. Along about this time Jane Murfin and Larry Trimble were searching and having the world searched for an unusual type of dog to be starred in a series of motion pictures. Hundreds were inspected and eliminated. Then they saw Etzel von Oeringen. They had found their dog. He was renamed "Strongheart."

Strongheart was three years old and weighed 115 pounds, his best fighting weight, when he arrived in the United States. He was a magnificent-looking animal, but had been so militantly trained that he was savage in both mood and actions. He was dangerous even for the men who handled him. He did not know how to walk like an ordinary dog. He marched like a soldier. He was a soldier. He was a highly trained military dog. A fighting cog in a thoroughly regimented national fighting machine.

Strongheart was formidable either in attack or defense. He had everything a military and police dog required—size, strength, speed, endurance, courage, fearlessness, agressiveness, catlike agility, and long, sharp fangs with which to hack and slash. From a crouching position he could leap over the head of a man six feet tall, and do it with what seemed to be effortless ease. That will give you some idea of the power he could turn on when necessary.

Strongheart's severe training had taken all the natural initiative and spontaneity out of him. He had no sense of fun, no joy, no affection, and did not know how to play. They had taken these things out of him in the process of turning him into a four-legged " dreadnought." Then Larry Trimble took over his education. Now it is always a significant event when Trimble takes over an animal for educational purposes, for he is a nonconformist of the first magnitude in his methods. Instead of the more or less conventional procedure in which a " superior " being compels an " inferior " one to follow certain traditional routines, Trimble treats his wild and domestic animal students as individual rational units, with unlimited capacities for development and accomplishment. It isn't a theory with him. He makes it work.

Some of his basic " secrets " are worth sharing, as they will help one understand some of the reasons for the dog's remarkable intelligence and his ability to do such extraordinary things. To begin with, Trimble has innumerable simple, almost childlike methods for winning first the interest, then the respect, and then the confidence of animals. All of them pivot around an effort to persuade the animals to turn immediately to him as their friend, whenever they are perplexed or afraid. Having accomplished this, he proceeds to find out just where he and the particular animal can meet on a basis of mutual understanding. Next, he carefully studies the animal's behavior patterns as well as its general attitudes towards life. With this information to work with, he begins releasing the animal from its inner and outer limitations, and helping it achieve its best possible development. In this tutoring Trimble makes everything a game for his four-legged students, and into these games he injects such easy lessons that the animals learn almost without effort.

Long experience has shown Trimble that every animal wants to be freindly with man, wants to coöperate with man, and will coöperate with man, whenever man does his part. He knows that every animal wants to think well of itself, wants to be understood, wants to be appreciated, and wants to find and be its best self. But he also knows how sensitive animals are to the mental atmosphere around them, and how arresting to their growth it is to hurt their feelings, to ridicule them, to nag at them, to laugh at them, to confuse them, to look down upon them with contempt, or to correct them in the wrong way. One of his basic rules is always to permit an animal to " save face "; that is, never to embarrass it, no matter what the animal may have done or neglected to do.

Trimble believes that one of the most harmful practices in animal education is the human habit of mentally limiting animals. He says that what the human thinks about an animal, and expects from an animal, has a direct bearing on the animal's response or lack of response. Should you ask him further, he will assure you that animals have a way of reading human minds with astonishing correctness. " When you are with an animal," Trimble once told me, " never be surprised when he does what you ask, even when you ask the first time. Always expect the impossible to happen. This will help you more than it does the animal. If there is no response, that is always a sign that you need more educating yourself. Not the animal."

Strongheart's re-education took many months of patient effort. He had to be de-regimented. He had to be made over inwardly. He had to be released from an assortment of bad behavior patterns drilled into him by narrow, limited, militantly minded humans. He had to be taught the meaning of love and friendship; how to play and have fun; how to care for others and be of service to them; how to do his own thinking; how to reason things out for himself; how to be in every way possible that which was rightly himself. The result of all this is now kennel and motion-picture history.

J. ALLEN BOONE.

# CONTENTS

# SUNBEAMS

*Hollywood*
*California*

*To*

*Strongheart*
*Eternal Playground*
*Out Yonder*

Dear old Pal:

Ever since they told me that you had suddenly changed your world, as the Japanese so quaintly express it, I have wanted to write to you and tell you some of the things that are in my mind and heart about us, things too intimate and deep to discuss with most human beings. I do not have to tell you that I am mentally standing by. You know that. Our friendship is geared for eternity; so whatever the seeming, nothing can get in between us and separate us. Nothing! I miss you very much, of course, but so does everyone else. And so does our little house, and your toys and games, and the Hollywood hills, and even that black cat across the street which seemed to take such a delight in climbing over the fence and making you chase it. But I know that all is well with you now and always. It has to be, for you are in, and part of, the great Eternal Plan.

Thin-souled people with sluggish imaginations and dimmed inner fires are saying that you are dead, buried and gone forever. "Strongheart is dead," they are assuring one another, "deader than a doornail! It's a pity, too, with all that popularity and the money he was earning for someone. Well, he may have been famous, but that didn't save him from having to die like all the rest of us. When his time came, he went like an ordinary dog. And that's the end of the famous Strongheart. I wonder if they've got another dog to take his place!" That's the way it goes. Chatter chatter, chatter! "Strongheart is dead!" I hear it everywhere. The newspapers and radio are proclaiming it to the ends of the earth. "Strongheart, the world's greatest animal actor, is dead!" They are saying it emphatically and with finality, like supreme court judges handing down irrevocable decisions.

I wish I could point a finger about the size of a lighthouse at all of them and shout, "Now listen, my funereal friends, I happen to be a very personal friend of Strongheart, and as his personal friend I should like to ask all of you just what you think that dog was made of? So many pounds of hide and bones and stuffings? A material body with something animating it on the inside, which has now stopped functioning? Well, if you do, you are mistaken. Very much so! You may have been looking at something like that, or at least thought you were, with those material eyes of yours, but what you were actually seeing were his qualities.

"That's what that dog was made of—qualities! Let me name a few of them for you: goodness . . . loyalty . . . understanding . . . enthusiasm . . . fidelity . . . devotion . . . sincerity . . . nobility affection . . . intelligence . . . honesty . . . confidence . . . strength . . . gentleness . . . happiness . . .

gratitude . . . appreciation . . . trustworthiness
. . . endurance . . . integrity . . . humility . . .
purity . . . unselfishness . . . fearlessness . . . love
. . . and all the hundreds of synonyms that parade
back of those terms.

"Qualities, my funereal friends! Grade One
qualities—even among the human species! Those
are the things he was made of, not that shadowy,
unsubstantial, phantom stuff called matter. But
qualities! Qualities of the highest excellence!
And write this down on the tablets of your
memories with the point of a diamond: those
qualities of Strongheart's can no more die and
be buried in a hole in the earth than a collection
of sunbeams. They are eternal! And Strongheart
is just as eternal as his qualities! Let me say that
just once more: Strongheart is just as eternal as
his qualities!"

At the moment you seem to be beyond my
human vision and the range of my whistle; and I
do not know how to throw the old tennis ball for
you, much as I would like to. But that is my fault.
All of us humans are more or less afflicted with
low and limited vision, which has a tendency to
give us distorted and contradictory notions about
what actually is and is not happening to the people
and things about us. We squint at life instead of
looking at it clear-eyed and steadily. We bend
our thinking processes inward and downward,
instead of upward and outward.

And that, according to the diagnosticians
among us, is why the human is in an almost continuous state of confusion; and why existence for
him seems to be such an irrational and unexplain-

able whirligig of birth and death, coming and going, success and failure, happiness and unhappiness, good and evil, and all the other contradictions peculiar to materiality. When the human is able to identify other forms of life within his immediate seeing range, he pronounces them "alive" and "in existence"; but when they do not happen to be within this narrow focus, he usually regards them as "dead" or "out of existence," and acts accordingly.

This is what the world of humans is doing to you now. They cannot identify you with their material senses; so, as far as they are concerned, you are dead, through, and out of existence for ever and ever. Had you been a human, they would have conceded that you probably had enough "something-or-other" to get you into some other kind of existence beyond this earthly one; but being only a dog, you will have to remain plain, ordinary, stationary dead. But there is a joker in the situation. I refuse to concur in the general verdict about you. I refuse to agree that you are either dead, through, or out of existence for ever and ever. I am voting *No* to the human world's *Yes*. It is a very tiny vote, considering the opposition's pile, but it is enough to keep that death verdict on you from becoming unanimous.

Let others believe you are dead if they desire; that is their privilege. But I want no part of it; for as far as I am concerned, you are just as vitally alive, and just as much the "old pal" now as ever. It could not be otherwise. I know too much about the expanse of the real you.

*I'll be seein' you*

4

## FOG

*To*

*Strongheart*
*Eternal Playground*
*Out Yonder*

Dear old Pal:

I am up as high as I can take myself geographically, mentally, and spiritually. From this vantage point I want to tell you once again why I am insisting that you *are* a great dog instead of *were* one. I started to write this in Hollywood, but the rumble of the biological treadmills was too disconcerting. I needed altitude—a place where fresh, clean winds would blow the smell of the genus *Homo* off me. I needed space, and solitude, and tranquility, where I could take the clamps off my thinking. So I got into my hiking clothes, slung the pack-bag on my back, selected an Irish walking stick, and here I am—atop the world.

This is just the kind of a place you would have selected. It is a high mountain meadow, and has everything a poet, a painter, a nature-lover, a boy, and a dog, would agree a mountain meadow ought to have. The view is magnificent in all directions: mountain ranges, valleys, cities, towns; in the distance, the Pacific Ocean; and back and far below me, the Mojave desert in a pastel make-up, spreading itself indolently in all directions. It is an ideal place in which to take a shot at the dreaded "Reaper whose name is Death," who is supposed to have sickled you out of existence, and to have separated us forever.

Death has always been humanity's most baffling and terrifying problem. It is our No. 1 enemy. Collectively speaking, we are so afraid of death, and so superstitious about it, that few have the courage to even question it, while investigating it at first hand is practically an unknown adventure. We are supposed to die as a sequence to having been born. So we die. We consent to die almost as readily as we expect to die. The routine of it goes like this: we arrive on this planet through a distressing process called birth. Then we struggle to an apex of years called maturity or old age. And then, unless otherwise bumped off, we go through a disintegrating process until we die and disappear.

What happens after death has been a matter of ground-and-lofty controversy for centuries. Some insist that death is a black, splotchy period at the end of a life sentence, marking the end. Others believe it to be a kind of stepping-stone in the direction of a more glorified state of existence, although they find it difficult understanding why it should be necessary to go through such a harrowing event as death in order to get there. Then there are those who regard the earth as a spinning, twirling reformatory, where mortals are cuffed and booted around by unseen corrective forces to prepare them for an unavoidable journey "through the valley of death" to a rewarding "heaven" or a punishing "hell," the destination depending to a great extent on their religious affiliations, and their personal conduct percentages according to the prevailing codes.

Let me illustrate: here is an average human in the midst of everyday existence. He did not ask to come here. As a matter of fact, he would probably have refused the invitation if it had been extended to him. Nevertheless, here he is, whether he likes it or not, doing the best he can with what he has to do it with. Life has not been particularly pleasant for him. His days have been filled with difficulties, disappointments, misfortunes, and sorrows. He has had little real happiness, and almost no fun. His outlook ahead is gloomy and depressing. Yet, in spite of all these things, he clings tenaciously, even desperately, to his sense of life. His problems threaten to overwhelm him. But he does not want to die out of them. He is afraid to, afraid that "the beyond" may be even more afflictive. So he struggles on with a heavy heart, hoping for the best, but expecting the worst.

Then, to quote an ancient hymn:

> Death enters and there's no defense—
> His time there's none can tell;
> He'll in a moment call thee hence
> To heaven or to hell.

The moment anything is born into what is known as "the earth life," "Death, the supreme Dictator," stamps the mark of doom upon it There are no exceptions. Every material life is predicted directly or indirectly on the expectancy

7

of death. Humans have been cringing and groveling before this "Grisly Terror" for centuries, treating it with ritualistic fear, veneration, and reverence. At least they have until comparatively recently. Now a revolution is under way, probably the most unusual revolution in all history. It began when a courageous and daring spiritual adventurer, with steady and far-reaching vision, walked boldly up to the apparition of death, and metaphorically threw a monkey-wrench into its ancient and elaborate machinery by proclaiming the whole process an out-and-out *lie*.

Other up-and-coming mental adventurers began rallying and heaving things too. The revolution was on. True, they have not routed death as yet. But it is not functioning nearly as well as it did. With complete disregard for traditional beliefs, these stout-hearted, clear-eyed, fearless revolutionists have declared death on death itself. "Down with death!" they are shouting mentally. "Death to death!" They intend to drive it entirely out of everyone's experience. Their strategy is unique. Instead of waiting for death to move in on them, they are moving in on death, equipped with the most powerful and potent of all weapons —*truth*. They are refusing to deal with death on its face value. Refusing to meet it on its own traditional grounds. They are refusing to let it frighten them. Or intimidate them. Instead they are doing a most unorthodox thing. They are laughing at death. Making fun of it. Thumbing their noses at it. Showing it no more respect than they would a big, ugly, potbellied bogeyman.

8

Death, say these irrepressible dissenters, is an utter fabrication! An illusion! A delusion! A gigantic, hideous hoax that has been played on mankind! "Don't be afraid of it!" they are shouting to their more timid fellows. "It cannot harm you. Or anyone. It has no power! No intelligence! No substance! No actual existence, except what you give it yourself in your individual belief. Death is plain nothing! A mirage! A bloated, historical myth made up of ignorance, fear, superstition, and mob mesmerism! It was not true when someone first imagined it long ago in the dark ages, and it is not true now."

How is that for putting death "on the spot"! It has had a tyrannical time for centuries. But its doom is sealed. The writing is on the wall. Already death is beginning to lose its terrifying importance. The deflation is under way. Humanity has at last begun to call its bluff.

From dawn until noon today I sat on a nearby peak, riding with the earth and "just a-lookin'." The more I watched those enchanting sweeps of earth and sky, the more unthinkable it became that a Creator capable of producing such exquisite loveliness would, or even could, make use of a revolting process like death for any purpose whatsoever. Such a thing was not only contrary to intelligence, but was preposterous. He couldn't possibly be that cruel, that wasteful, that stupid.

Towards noon a fog rolled in from the Pacific Ocean and began blotting out the landscape below me. First the coast resorts disappeared; then the nearer cities and towns and valleys; then the mountains, until all that remained of the universe was a nearby peak, part of the mountain meadow, and me. What an apt illustration of the phenomenon of death, I thought. Death is no more than fog which has rolled in and temporarily shut off one's view. But for inward assurance that it wasn't true, everything on earth was "dead and gone" as far as my material senses were concerned. I had no way of proving otherwise from where I was looking out at things. I knew, though, that the fog was impermanent, and that on the other side of the mist life was going on just as vigorously as ever—whether my human senses subscribed to it or not. There is nothing to be afraid of in a fog, I told myself. One can always get through a fog with the right compass directions and careful navigation. Fog is not an obstruction. It is merely temporary obscuration from the observer's point of view. Or better still, *in* his point of view. And that is just what death is being found out to be—temporary obscuration *in* the observer's point of view.

I will admit that the fog of death seems to have rolled in between us and to have separated us from one another. But the important point is this: it cannot get into my thinking and affections, where you have lived ever since I met you. Nothing in there can ever harm you, or break the bond of love and understanding between us. And that, old Pal, is why I know that all is well with you— and us.

*I'll be seein' you*

# BLUE SKIES

*Sierra Madre Mountains
California*

*To*

*Strongheart
Eternal Playground
Out Yonder*

Dear old Pal:

After a number of delectable days on top of these mountains, following unfrequented paths to see where they were going and what they did when they got there, I am about to set my feet moving in the direction of the Mojave desert via cattle and coyote trails. But before I leave, I want to take one more pot shot at the ill-boding phenomenon of death. I will do it on behalf of both of us, as we are supposed to be on opposite sides of the thing; that is, popular belief has you listed as a "dead dog" and me as a "living human." Well, let's see about it, before I sling the old pack on my back.

Death, let me say again, is humanity's most baffling and dreaded enigma. It has been accepted with resignation by almost everyone as an unavoidable part of life on earth. "How did such a horrible thing as death ever get into experience?" humans ask one another with grief-filled, quaking hearts. "Why do we have to die? What good does it do? What does it accomplish? We come to know and love people here, and then they are snatched from us—often in the most terrible ways. Why? And what happens to them in the experience of death? Is that the end of them? Or is there a better state of existence after this one? If there is, does everyone go there? Or only favoured ones? And what about all the four-legged animals, and the birds, and the insects, and such things? Where do they go after they die? Or don't they! Do humans have a better opportunity than other forms of life, in whatever follows the present state of existence? Where at this moment are all the people who have died? And the four-legged animals? Shall we ever see them again? And, if so, will they be the same as they were here?"

When questions like these come at me aggressively, I usually find a quiet place, get as calm inwardly as I can, and go through a process we humans call "reasoning," thinking this way and that way, up hill and down hill, around familiar and strange corners, until I arrive at some kind of a satisfying conclusion. I move into it something like this:

I say to myself, "Well, no matter what seems to be going on around me, or happening to me, at least I can think. And thank God for that! I have a mind. All kinds of things are happening in my mind. I am aware of them. I can identify them. I can distinguish between them. That makes me a thinker. As a thinker I am equipped to do quite remarkable things. For instance, I can think in circumferences of fractions of an inch. Or I can open up and expand my thinking to include planets so far away that no one can put together terms adequate to describe the distance. I can think when I please, what I please, as I please. I can think upward or downward, to right or to left, forward or backward, constructively or destructively, pleasantly or disagreeably. It is my mind! And I am the thinker!

"This being so means that whatever seems to be happening throughout the length and breadth of the universe is taking place within the borders of my individual mind or consciousness. Inside my mind, not outside of it. Were they happening outside of my mind, how could I possibly know anything about them? Then this universe that I see all about me is internal, not external. The universe does not include me. On the contrary, I include the universe. The whole cosmic setup is inside my mind! Inside me! Part of my mind! Part of me! *Me*, in fact!

" 'But what about the people and things that your material senses report as detached objects moving around "out there" and "over yonder"?' asks something-or-other from somewhere-or-other. Mental concepts, I assure myself. Mental concepts within the borders of my own mind. Mental concepts in my own personal world of awareness, and so subject to the influence of my thinking. I used to reason out as far as this and then hit a snag—my material body. And the snag was this: was I on the inside of my material body? Or was my material body inside of me? Was I stuffed inside skin boundaries that had to be held up by a skeleton? Or was the whole thing a concept in my own mind?"

The generally accepted belief is that we humans

13

live inside our skin bodies; that we are in there with a peculiar assortment of gadgets which enable us to navigate them around in a limited sort of way. Inclosed in these skin casings we are supposed to get information from the "outside world" through the senses of sight, hearing, touch, smell, and taste. I was taught this as a youngster and was supposed not to question it as I grew older. And I didn't for a long time. But the thing puzzled me, bothered me. I could not understand how it was possible for me to live in such a damp, dark, disagreeable, disillusioning, badly arranged, badly ventilated, and uninviting place as the inside of a human body. Nor could I reason out how it was I knew so much about the outside of my body while I was supposed to be imprisoned within the thing. It did not seem to make good sense.

Then one day a wise and experienced spiritual traveller told me a startling and unforgettable thing. This: that I did not live inside my material body at all. But outside of it. Completely outside of it. Said he: "That skin contraption you call your body is yours, but not you. Keep that distinction sharply in mind if you want to get anywhere in existence. Your body is yours. But not you. It is no more you—that is, the real you—than your overcoat, or your automobile, or your fountain pen. You are consciousness. You are a mental not a physical, being. That which you have been calling your body is a mental concept. It may appear to be physical substance. It may seem to be and feel very real. But sooner or later you will be compelled, in one way or another, to realize

14

that it is a mental concept, a formation of your own thinking, and so subject to your own thinking."

That was one of the most helpful things anyone ever told me. With it I can spread out to enormous proportions. With it I can assure myself that I am as high, as wide, as deep, and as inclusive as I can think. As I can imagine! And I can say it with cosmic humility, too. Now, I was never conscious of being born into material existence. They tell me I was. And I seem to be here with a material body. But I have no recollection at all of that birth experience, except from hearsay. That I shall ever die out of material existence is extremely doubtful, and for what seems to me to be a very simple reason. Death is supposed to be a complete cessation of mental and physical functioning. If my mental functioning stops, how am I to know that I am experiencing death? How can I go through the process of dying and at the same time know about it? Obviously it is an impossible feat.

That, it would appear, reduces the whole matter to this: I do not do any dying myself. It has to be the other fellow. Always the other fellow. Not me. I have to keep alive to do the thinking about it. No thinking about it on my part, then no dying by the other fellow on his part. Unless I am vitally there with my thinking to say so, there can be no dying or death anywhere. I am my own universe, my own mental universe. I can know and experience only what goes on in this universe. So that puts the whole question of death squarely up to me as an individual thinker.

There can be no evasion, no quibbling. For me to be able to identify anyone or anything, the person or thing must be in my individual world of awareness, in my own mind, or consciousness. Being in there, I am responsible for them, for I am the one who does the thinking about them.

That places an enormous obligation on me, doesn't it! It means that if anyone dies, he goes through the process within the areas of my own mind, or consciousness, over which I am supposed to rule supreme. I am the one who has to say that someone is dying for it to be a fact, as far as I am concerned. I put the death sentence on him. I pronounce him dead. I break the connections between us. I dig the grave and cover him up. Or cremate him. I rule that he has disappeared from my experience, probably forever. It all goes on within the borders of my own mind, or consciousness. With my consent. With my approval. With my help. A ghastly business, isn't it! Now it seems logical that if I should persist in such mentally destructive, mortuary practices, only one thing can happen. I shall transform this individual world of awareness of mine into a vast cemetery, filled with decaying, dying, and dead concepts about a Creation which God, in the beginning, is reported to have pronounced "very good."

Now about you and me. Once upon a time you did not exist as far as I was concerned. Then suddenly you arrived in my world of awareness. You became an important part of my consciousness of existence. An important part of me. You brought with you one of the finest companionships

16

I have ever known. But you did more than that. You taught me new meanings of happiness . . . of devotion . . . of honour . . . of individuality . . . of loyalty . . . of sincerity . . . of love . . . of life . . . of God. And now just because feeble, limited human senses are unable to identify that material body of yours, I am supposed to join in a traditionally barbarous procedure, and hang a death tag on one end of you and a burial certificate on the other. Imagine treating a pal like that! Especially a pal like you!

You dead? Well, if you are, it did not happen within the latitudes and longitudes of my thinking areas. I would not permit such a thing. And I know you would do as much for me. You dead? Preposterous! You and I know too much about life, don't we!

*I'll be seein' you*

## DESERT RAT

*Mojave Desert*
*California*

*To*

*Strongheart*
*Eternal Playground*
*Out Yonder*

Dear old Pal:

Yipped at by coyotes, hooted at by owls, and barked at by ranch dogs, I came down from the mountains last night. A full moon, which filled the countryside with weird and fascinating shadowgraphs, made it possible for me to see the trail. At the moment I am quite some distance out in the Mojave desert. It is high noon—not a cloud in the sky, and no shade. Just dazzling sunshine and oven heat. I am sitting here, flanked on one side by a lone-some cactus, and on the other by some ominous-looking bleached bones, waiting for a friend of mine. His name is Mojave Dan, and he is probably the most nomadic two-legged thing moving around on the surface of this desert. What I am attempting to do is to deflect the swing of his present orbit in this direction so that I can join him.

Selecting this spot as a rendezvous was one of two things—inspiration or lunacy, depending on results. It is difficult to imagine anyone coming to this place for any purpose. While looking over an old map, I saw the name Red Butte, and presumed it to be one of those high elevations in the desert from which Indians probably flashed smoke signals years ago. When I arrived here the butte turned out to be nothing more than an overgrown reddish sandpile. Or maybe I am at the wrong butte.

Well, right or wrong, here I am. I sent word in the general direction of Dan that I would be waiting for him at this spot, but have no means of knowing whether or not he received the message. Even if he did, it may be that he has never heard of this out-of-the-way sandpile. The letter was sent via a special grape-vine made up of stage drivers, prospectors, ranchers, miners, and rangers, all of whom know Dan. If it reached him, he ought to make his appearance some time today. If it didn't, I shall have to trek back over long stretches of desert and begin all over again.

I always wanted you and Dan to meet and get to know one another, but could never arrange it, as the desert was too hot for you, and Dan refuses to come out of the desert. He does not like cities or citified people. They taint his disposition, he says. Dan is a desert rat. That term is very elastic, but generally speaking it means a man who has become so enamoured of the desert that he would not, and probably could not, live anywhere else and be contented. Most desert rats are easy-going, foot-loose explorers for gold and other mineral deposits; and as a class they are unsurpassed in picturesqueness and originality. That goes double for Dan.

He came into the desert years ago with a college

education back of him, a theoretical knowledge of mining, and ambitions to become the world's richest man. But gradually the desert turned his academic sense of values upside down and inside out, as the desert has a way of doing to its converts. Little by little he began giving up his success formulas, his interest in material gain, and his ambitions to be thought important among the human species; he followed and did whatever his fancy suggested. In other words, he became a desert rat.

Dan could be a rich man if he desired, but he doesn't so desire. He knows where there are valuable gold deposits tucked away in the earth, but he pans only enough of it to pay for the modest upkeep of his animals and himself. Dan believes that wealth interferes with the enjoyment of life, as it takes one's interest away from the simpler and more satisfying things, and robs him of his peace of mind. If you measured him by city standards, Dan's rating would be about zero, for his only tangible assets are some old patched clothes, a few animals with only sentimental value, and a weather-beaten, much-travelled camping outfit.

He has been called shiftless, irresponsible, and eccentric. There are those who say he is quite mad; but as he regards most human opinions as entirely without value, these unfavourable judgments become meaningless as far as he is concerned. In spite of his lack of social and financial standing, however, Dan is one of the wealthiest men in the world. He is rich in the things that the rest of the world would like to possess, if it only knew how.

For instance, Dan has almost complete freedom in thought and action. He has no economic problems. He goes wherever he wants to go, whenever he desires. When he gets there, he does what he wants to do, in the way he likes to do it. He is not bound or influenced by people . . . things . . . events . . . or circumstances. His contentment is continuous. Nothing worries him. And he knows neither disappointment nor regret.

Dan makes practical use of the wise-dog philosophy that life is something to be appreciated, lived, and enjoyed today. Now! At this very minute. Dan is a minute man. He concentrates the whole of himself on the present minute, living it fully and completely and permitting the hours, days, weeks, months, years, and centuries to shift for themselves. He does not struggle with existence. He has a better way. He keeps his attitudes flexible and friendly, and flows along with the universe. Yes, he is crazy—like the birds and the flowers.

It was Dan who gave me my first real clue to you. I knew very little about dogs when I met you. True, we became sleeping partners and shared existence together, but even these intimacies did not seem to get me any closer to what seemed to be another and more important you, back of the material you. You kept me in an almost continuous state of confusion. You knew altogether too much for a dog. At least I thought so. You were too intelligent. Too wise. It embarrassed me. I knew how to feed and bathe you, how to keep the fleas off your distinguished hide, and how to give you your daily workouts, as these instructions had been written down for me as though for a child; but the more I was with you, the more baffling you became.

I wanted to know where you got your intelligence . . . your keen powers of observation . . . and your remarkable intuition. I wanted to know why it was that so many of your instincts and capacities surpassed mine in actual performance. I wanted to know how you read the character and intentions of human beings so accurately. How you anticipated events so unerringly. I read every available dog book, and consulted all kinds of so-called dog experts; but none of them explained you. I found out a great deal about breeding, training, and exhibiting dogs; much about their outsides, but very little about their insides. And I was interested in your insides. Not your organic insides; but in that mysterious elusive, intangible something-or-other which gave you your identity . . . flavoured you . . . moved your material body around . . . and made you "the world's greatest dog."

My quest took me around in circles, but then all the so-called experts seemed to be going around in circles themselves. I knew vaguely that you consisted of a great deal more than I was looking at with my material eyes. I also had a constantly growing conviction that all of you dogs were of far greater importance in the universal design of life than human beings have even begun to discover yet. But how to get at it? How to break through centuries of squeaky old beliefs about dogs? One night the idea came to me to ask Dan. He usually knows all the right answers.

I left at dawn, drove through canyons, over mountains, across valleys, and by the greatest good fortune found him in his favourite little desert town replenishing his supplies. I laid the problem of you before him. He listened patiently like an old family lawyer. Then he said, "There's facts about dogs, and there's opinions about dogs. The dogs have the facts, and the humans the opinions. If you want the facts, get them from the dogs; if you want the opinions, get them from the humans."

That is all there was to it, but that was enough. I knew instantly where I had been making my mistake. And that, my dear Strongheart, explains how you happened to get me as a pupil. Dan says that it was the most sensible thing he ever knew me to do.

*I'll be seein' you*

## BURROS

*Mojave Desert*
*California*

*To*

*Strongheart*
*Eternal Playground*
*Out Yonder*

Dear old Pal:

All's well! Dan got my letter, knew the location of Red Butte, and here we are together. From now on I am an apprentice desert rat. The sun was nearing the horizon when I caught sight of him yesterday. He and his burros and his dogs were snaked-out for at least half a mile. Far ahead and acting as chief scout was "The Sheriff," part wolf and part Airedale. Some distance behind him was "Mike," an amusing but temperamental Irish terrier. At his heels was "Lobo," a mixture of greyhound and sheep-dog, and a great companion in rough country. Then came Dan, shuffling along in his relaxed, easy way; and last of all marched the four burros—"Madame X," "Willie," "Jerry," and "Little Jonathan."

They arrived at sundown, and after the usual greetings Dan started the evening meal over a fire of brushwood. He did very well considering where we were and what he had in the way of cooking utensils. The menu? Tomato soup, bacon

24

and beans, fried potatoes and onions, hot biscuits and honey, and a special cake he "threw together" for the occasion, made of dates, nuts, quick-rising batter, and something he shook out of a sun-blued glass. Then coffee. Dan is noted for his coffee. It is a powerful but tasty brew, which he makes in an old battered pot with ritualistic mystery. He says the secret of his good coffee lies in a chunk of iron which he drops into the pot with the coffee, and which floats to the top when the brew is ready.

After supper we rolled into our blankets, with the Mojave for our bed, looked at the stars, and talked. Then I fell asleep. How long this lasted I do not know, but I was suddenly awakened by something striking me in the face. We were in the midst of a sandstorm. Imagine that! A sandstorm at that whatever-it-was hour of the night! It had hit us with force and fury. I covered my head with my blanket and lay as flat to the earth as I could. Two of the dogs shoved their heads under the blanket with me and quaked. Camp gear flew over us, around us, and caromed off us. Once I ventured to look out through a narrow slit in my blanket. The air was filled with flying sand. A pan, looking as big as a washtub, shot past my head and bounded off in the general direction of the Atlantic seaboard.

Then I saw the burros. The storm was hitting them from the front, the rear, from above, and from below. But it did not seem to be disturbing them in the least. They were standing like statues, with their eyes closed and their ears folded back against their necks. They were displaying perfect self-possession, tranquility, and patience. When the blow was over, Dan and I crawled out of our blankets to make an appraisal of ourselves and the camp gear. We were perturbed emotionally and physically. I happened to look in the direction of the burros. They had unfolded their ears, and were looking at us two humans calmly but with what appeared to be amused interest. They had weathered the storm much better than either of us, and evidently they felt a little superior about it.

I said to Dan, "How is it those burros behaved so much better in that blow than you did? I thought burros were supposed to be stupid."

"Well, for one thing," Dan replied, "they have less ego than I have, and so they haven't as many things to be afraid of. For another, they are more sensible. They know that trouble never lasts, no matter in what form it comes. So they don't fight it. They just fold back their ears, and let the trouble fight itself. They keep out of it. They are too smart to meet physical force with physical force. They may run into a heap of trouble, but they never seem to let it get inside of them. Nothing disturbs their poise. They have learned the art of non-resistance."

I thought about this, as Dan started out to hunt for blown-away camp gear. When he came back, I asked him if he knew that many of the world's greatest thinkers were advocating intelligent non-resistance as the most effective method for solving individual and collective problems. If he heard me, he gave no indication. I talked on just as though he had. One does that with Dan.

"These great thinkers," I continued, "say that non-resistance, with understanding, tolerance, and love, not only conserves mental and phsyical energy, but removes all barriers to a happy and successful existence."

Dan snorted. "The burros have been practicing that ever since they started to walk the earth," he flung back at me. "Those wise human beings may know how to talk about things like that, but the burros know how to live them. And you'd better get over that notion that burros are stupid. There's a lot that you and I could learn from them right now. Don't ever forget that. And let me tell you this, too: the burro is so intelligent that it takes uncommon intelligence on the part of a human being to appreciate its intelligence.

"The burro has been misunderstood and misrepresented for years. And I'll tell you why. First of all, it refuses to be bossed, or bluffed, or intimidated by human beings; and when human beings can't do these things to others, they are apt to get mean and spiteful. That's just what they did to the burros. Human beings crave to have others plan and manage their lives for them. But not the burro. He is an individualist. He wants to live his life in his own way. He objects to being told what to do, and how to do it. He is friendly, and he likes to co-operate; but he is against being dominated.

"The world calls the burro perverse, when he is only respecting his independence. It calls him obstinate, when he is simply standing up boldly for his own rights—like any other American citizen. It calls him ornery, when he is merely resolute of purpose. He is a dissenter, of course; but he has to be, or others would take advantage of him. And remember, it's the dissenters and the objectors who have kept the world from crystallising. If this country did what it should have done long ago, it would knock that eagle off its perch as the national emblem, and give that honorary job to the one it belongs to—the burro."

"Why, what's wrong with the eagle?" I asked.

"Plenty!" he snorted. "The eagle is a trouble-maker. It's a disturber. A murderer. Almost every-thing it does is destructive. It likes to be cruel. It likes to kill. It has bad morals. And worse manners. It is conceited, mean, treacherous, greedy, and selfish."

There was much more in the indictment, but I could not distinguish all of it as Dan was moving about looking for pots and pans, and scattering his talk in all directions. I crawled into my blanket again. Dan's voice went on and on. He was in a talking mood. Much of his oration had to do with the gallant part the burros played in helping conquer and build up the great American West. It was good stuff, but not good enough to keep me from dozing.

Now and then his vocal climaxes would arouse me somewhat. In one of them he exclaimed with dramatic fervour, "The burros didn't need those pioneers, but the pioneers certainly needed the burros. What would they have done without them in this country?" There being no answer from me, he shouted, "Nothing!" Then after a pause he added, "And let me tell you this as historical fact. If those pioneers had behaved themselves as

28

well as the burros, the United States wouldn't be having all the trouble it has today. The burros had the real moral and social codes. Not the pioneers."

Gradually his words fused into meaningless sounds. And the sounds became a droning accompaniment for something else. Something that chanted rhythmically through my sleepy thoughts—like this:

*When storms blow in*
*And "do their stuff,"*
*And the going's rough*
*And things look tough—*
*Fold back your ears and wait.*

*Don't fight trouble*
*On trouble's own level;*
*That is always unwise.*
*Fold back your ears and wait.*

*Don't worry and fret so,*
*You funny little man.*
*Difficulties never last*
*And they have no real substance.*
*Fold back your ears and wait.*

*Be quiet and calm inside*
*And all will come out right.*
*It has to. That is the Law. So*
*Fold back your ears and wait.*

*And when the trouble blows away,*
*As troubles always do—*

29

*Unfold your ears and go on.*
*That's the trick, little man.*

It must have been the burros coming through on a more powerful wave-length than Dan's.

*I'll be seein' you*

## HIGH ADVENTURE

*Mojave Desert*
*California*

*To*

*Strongheart*
*Eternal Playground*
*Out Yonder*

Dear old Pal:

Since my last letter Dan, the dogs, the burros, and I have moved over many miles of desert. We are now camped near an old deserted house, where once upon a time someone watched a dream of wealth expand and explode. Not far away is a mine which should have been rich in gold deposits but wasn't. We arrived late at night. As we approached the house, I was stopped in my tracks. Two empty chairs on the front porch were slowly rocking back and forth, as though occupied by invisible people enjoying the loveliness of the desert night. It made cold shivers run up and down my spine. As we started toward the porch, the chairs stopped rocking. We stopped, too, in bewildered surprise. Then the chairs started rocking again. We charged forward. It took us some time to solve the mystery, but finally we did. The chairs were so well balanced on their rockers that the slightest current of air set them in motion. What a story those two old chairs could tell!

Dan and I are in the midst of a bed-time story contest. Each night after we roll into our blankets one of us tells a story. If the other is awake at the end of it, the narrator gets one thousand points; otherwise he loses that amount. Up until last night Dan had won all the points, having gone to sleep, or pretended to, in the middle of one of my stories. I am unable to work this trick on him, as he has a way of injecting sudden and quite blood-curdling sound effects into his talks, whether they fit in or not, which always set me straight up as though something had booted me from below. Dan is a "slicker" in things like this.

Last night, however, I changed my tactics. I dropped my city-flavoured stories and told him about that never-to-be-forgotten adventure of ours on Pine Ridge. Let me recall it, as I always love rethinking it. We had been in the mountains all day, and late in the afternoon you found that delectable ridge with the far-flung views, where we had supper and watched the sun go down. Then you turned yourself into a pillow, and I laid my head on your comfortable, flexible ribs and watched the stars appear. It was an unusually brilliant night overhead, and as I lay there I got to wondering about stars. How did they come into being in the first place? Of what were they made? What held them up there? How did they manage to move at such incredible speed? What guided them so unerringly? How was it that the celestial traffic was managed so much better than the terrestrial?

There seemed to be only one answer. Something

up there was not only directing everything with great judgment and skill, but was doing so with superb artistry. I was looking at flawlessly managed co-ordination and control. Gradually I began to sense that the same power which was moving and managing things so effectively in the heavens was also at work all about me. The whole universe was pulsating with life and loveliness. Nothing was haphazard anywhere. Infinite activity . . . law . . . order . . . purpose . . . precision . . . rhythm . . . and excellence of the highest order were everywhere.

Life began taking on new meaning. It dawned on me that I was not merely a human being inside skin dimensions, laid out on a mountain ridge, and looking out through two holes in my head at a glittering pageant millions of light years away. I was part of the performance myself. I, too, was a member of the great Cosmic cast. All Creation was dancing. And so was I, even though my material body was as motionless as a log. I was dancing with a more expansive part of me, a part that was not restricted by material conditions. I was prancing all over Creation with everything else, limited only by the bounds of my imagination.

Quite suddenly mountains, rocks, trees, and stars stopped being material objects. Instead they became signs, symbols, and manifestations of great and enduring verities back of them. They became individualized and friendly expressions of a primal Mind of supreme and infinite proportions. A Mind which included them all. A Mind which governed them all. A Mind which controlled them all. I knew what was happening to me. I was beginning to get firsthand glimpses of the realities "behind the shadowy shapes of things that seem to be."

I could sense a lovely Presence moving quietly, gently, but irresistibly through everything near and far. "Why, all this that I am seeing, and feeling, and otherwise experiencing is God!" I gasped to myself. "God is not something across distance! Something 'way off there'! Or 'far out yonder'! Or hard to get to! Or difficult to understand and blend with! God is everywhere present! Even more so than the very air I am breathing! I am in a perfectly functioning, really marvellous Creation! A necessary part of it! And so is everyone and everything else! We are all in the great Cosmic design and purpose together. All parts of a vast, inseparable, harmonious Togetherness! All related to one another! All needed to make the Whole complete!"

At that moment you rolled from under me, sat up, and began staring at me with those deep, penetrating eyes of yours. Then if ever a dog talked, you did. There were no words to it, no sounds in your throat, no physical movement. It was language too spacious for such limitations. Said you, "So you have discovered that you are part of a great Creation, have you? That's fine. But what about me? Where do I fit into it? And all the other dogs? And all the other animals? Are we supposed to be in the same God-design and plan as you humans? Are we supposed to be under the same God-management as you? Or do

34

you humans have special privileges from which the rest of us are excluded?"

"Yes, and then again, no!" I thought back at you, wondering how you could introduce involved questions on such a beautiful night. "No human would dispute the fact that you dogs and all the rest of the animals are in Creation. But as to your being related to the same God-source, and under the same God-management as the humans claim for themselves, that is a controversial matter, and when I say this I am speaking of my species collectively. A general vote would probably result in an overwhelming '*No.*' The popular belief is that all of you four-leggers were placed in the universe for the convenience and use of human beings. And that gives you a minus rating right from the start.

"And speaking on behalf of those who divide life into 'human beings' and 'lower forms of life,' let me ask just what you dogs and the rest of the animals are supposed to be doing in the universe anyway? Aside from those of you that we can chase, shoot, eat, ride, or otherwise use to our advantage, of what use are you? Why should any of you be necessary in a world owned and controlled by human beings, a world in which humans fill all the important places, and are capable of doing all the needful things? We humans could easily invent substitutes for everything you animals are or contribute to the scheme of things."

I knew I wasn't going to get away with anything like that with you. And I didn't. You had a discomforting way of seeming to look straight through people at times, and that was one of those occasions.

Again you spoke in that silent but impressive way of yours, and what I caught of it was this, "Just how important or necessary anything is in Creation is not for any human to decide. That right belongs exclusively to the Creator. Human capacities are too shallow and limited for such authority. And besides, you humans are too muddled about the meaning and purpose of Creation. Would you like to know what confuses you? Trying to look down at Creation from what you believe to be your superior elevation. When you do this, your vanity makes shadows of your conceits, and hides the truth from you. To see and understand Creation you have to look out *with* it. You cannot break up Creation into parts. You cannot be exclusive. If you humans are connected with a Source of life and intelligence greater than your own, so are all the rest of us. If you are part of an eternal plan, so are we. We are all in this adventure of life together. I need you. But you need me. And we all need one another."

Then you gave my face a couple of licks, barked lustily, and started off in the general direction of Hollywood. You had issued your orders. I threw the pack together, slung it on my back, and trailed along after you—a wiser and better human.

It took some time to say vocally all I have set down briefly in this letter. When I finished, I looked over at Dan. He was actually awake, eyes wide open, looking up at the stars. He made no comment at all. Instead he did an unusual thing. He rolled out of his blankets, made a pot of coffee, and we drank it without either of us saying a word. I had won my first one thousand points in the contest.

*I'll be seein' you*

# INDIANS

*Mojave Desert*
*Caliornia*

*To*

*Strongheart*
*Eternal Playground*
*Out Yonder*

Dear old Pal:

There are now three additions to our vagabond outfit, an Indian named Little Beaver, and his two dog-companions Long Trail and Bright Water. Dan and Little Beaver have been friends for many years. Liking one another's company, they manage to make their trails converge two or three times each year. Then they wander about the desert together. This is one of those occasions. For the time being we are camping in a rather small oasis far off the regular trails, where there is a spring, trees, shade, and an abundance of tranquility. It is great fun travelling with this unusual pair of humans. During the daytime we scarcely ever speak to one another, unless it is absolutely necessary. This is part of the unwritten code of the desert. The rule is to see and hear all you can, think all you wish to, but talk as little as possible.

Little Beaver, who is one of the quietest and wisest men I have ever known, says that talking spills one's power. Dan thoroughly endorses this, adding that he has yet to find a man capable of talking well enough to improve on desert silence. The only time this talking ban is off is early in the morning when we discuss plans for the day, and from the evening meal until we go to sleep. We are a rare-looking caravan on the march. There is no pace-setting; each of us moves in his own style and at whatever speed he fancies.

The dogs always run far ahead on self-appointed scouting duty. Then comes Dan, with his hat pulled down to shade his eyes, walking with an easy-going shuffle peculiar to desert rats. Little Beaver is usually a third or a quarter of a mile behind him, walking as though he did not want to disturb the earth with his moccasined feet. The burros follow one another some distance behind Little Beaver. I march just back of the last burro, by choice. It is the best position for observation purposes; and besides, whenever I desire to do so, I can hang on to the burro's tail and get towed—a trick I learned from camel boys in Egypt.

The dogs are the best travellers in our caravan. They get over the ground better, they see more, and they have more fun. In spite of the heat and the rough going they always find something to interest them every inch of the way. I know their secret, though, thanks to my training with you. They carry their happiness with them on the inside, and spill it over everything. They do not hunt adventure. They create it as they go along. Outward conditions never seem to interrupt the gushing of their inward enthusiasm and expectancy of good. On the trail they run back

39

frequently to reassure us of their continuing affection. I think they are sorry for the rest of us, because of our physical inability to keep up with them. Their energy, enthusiasm, joy, appreciation, and gratitude for the privilege of living are an inspiration.

Like all you dogs, they have mastered the art of being able to get entertainment and satisfaction out of practically nothing at all. They live each moment fully and completely. They do nothing half-heartedly or indifferently. Yesterday, for instance, we crossed miles of dull, tedious desert. It really was not the kind of climate or country for any dog to be in. And yet they made the hot wastelands yield them rich dividends in enjoyment all the way. They refused to permit life to become monotonous even on a monotonous desert.

Now let me tell you about Little Beaver, as you two would like one another in a big way. According to the way humans segregate and label their races, Little Beaver is an Indian, or Red man. Dan and I are classified as White men. Little Beaver's father was a great chief, a man much respected throughout the Indian nation for his wisdom and moral integrity. For many generations he and his ancestors lived in the Western part of the United States, building a civilization on fine ethical, social, and esthetic foundations. Their system of government was better planned and managed than most of those in use throughout the world today. They were a free, contented, happy, spiritually minded people.

Then an ominous cloud appeared in the

East. The White man's civilization, with its ruthless acquisitiveness, was moving Westward—grabbing, grabbing, grabbing. Eventually the leaders discovered that the Indians were living on lands rich in minerals and oils and valuable for other purposes. Something had to be done about that. And something was done. Pretending to have the Indians' interests at heart, and screening their greedy ambitions back of fake patriotism and self-righteous cant, the White men ganged up on the Red men with the latest devices in slaughtering instruments, and gave them what is technically known in gangster circles as "the works."

There was courageous, brilliant resistance by the Indians, but the White men had an overwhelming advantage in numbers and armament. When the fighting was over, the White men were in possession of the Indian's land. And the Indians? Well, those that escaped being killed were herded together like cattle and placed in open-air prisons called reservations. Once again the White man and his civilization had triumphed.

Dan has strong convictions about that period of Western history. He says it would have been much better for the United States if the Indians had conquered the White men. The Indians, he insists, had a better and more practical knowledge of individual and group living. Says Dan, and I omit the sulphurous phrases which went with it, "The White men took the Indian's land. But they weren't smart enough to take his wisdom, or his culture, or his virtues, or his ideas about community living, or his laws, or his government.

They just took the land, and by way of exchange gave the Indians an assortment of bad examples, diseases, vices, misery—and cooped them up in reservations."

Little Beaver bears no resentment, though. He is too wise for that. Years ago he was shipped away from his reservation with other Indians to be educated in the manner of the White men. But it did not work out at all well. In the first place, he was not accustomed to living within four walls. To add to this, he did not like the manners, the morals, the social codes, or the thinking processes of his paleface teachers. He considered them much inferior to those of his own people. He tried to be a good student, but when his keen senses observed that his teachers were not living the things they were trying to teach him, he ran away and returned to the desert, where he understood everything and everything understood him.

In spite of his lack of what White men call "schooling." Little Beaver is one of the best-educated men I have ever met. What he knows goes far beyond conventional academic boundaries. He is very religious, too. And this in spite of the fact that he has never talked with a clergyman, has never been in a church, and knows almost nothing about religious organizations, creeds, or articles of faith. His religion is as natural and as much a part of him as his breathing. It consists almost entirely of an endeavour to be constantly aware of the all-pervading presence of the Great Spirit, and to move in harmony with It.

Little Beaver is credited with all kinds of

mysterious powers, because of his ability to see, hear, and know about things beyond the capacities of most humans. He never reads books, magazines, or newspapers. He rarely asks questions. He talks very little. Yet his ability to understand what has happened, is happening, or is going to happen, is amazing. He reads intentions in people as though they were made of glass, and he reads them even before the people appear physically. I know his secret, though. I know how he does these things. I can say it in three words: purification, prayer, receptivity.

For instance, whenever Little Beaver needs information, advice, or help, he always uses the same method. He first cleanses his body. Then he empties his mind of everything he believes shouldn't be there. Then he goes to the quietest and most beautiful spot he can find, puts himself in rapport with the Great Spirit, and listens. He listens humbly, patiently, trustingly, and expectantly for the Great Spirit to tell him what to do, and how to do it. The favourite time for this is just before dawn. His favourite place, any elevation facing the rising sun. During these periods of communion with the Great Spirit he goes without food and water, in order to sharpen his receptive faculties.

His prayers consist almost entirely of thanksgiving and listening. He never attempts to impress, or flatter, or advise the Great Spirit. He never begs for favours; he never asks for special privileges for himself. Instead he subordinates everything to his inner hearing, his inner vision. When he receives his instructions from the Great Spirit, he acts immediately. If, say, he or some of his friends have lost cattle, he will return from his prayers knowing why the cattle disappeared, where they are, who is involved in it, and the best way to handle the situation. He never follows earth trails, but always inner guidance.

Yesterday I asked him how he knew a certain prospector was going to cross our trail at a certain place and hour, long before we met him. He shrugged his shoulders, smiled, and said, "In-knowing!" That is all the explanation he would give me. I asked Dan how he would define "in-knowing" if I asked him as one gentleman to another.

"Well, you could define it in a lot of different ways," he said. "You could call it intuition, or immediate perception, or instant discernment, or direct knowing, or insight, or a 'hunch.' They all mean about the same thing—the sudden arrival in a little mind of something from the Big Mind."

"Do you suppose the great prophets of the past meant the same thing when they spoke of 'the voice of God' coming to them?" I asked.

"Certainly!" said Dan. "Only they were smart enough to listen and follow directions."

"Like Little Beaver?" I asked.

Dan nodded.

*I'll be seein' you*

44

# RATTLESNAKES

*Mojave Desert*
*California*

*To*

*Strongheart*
*Eternal Playground*
*Out Yonder*

Dear old Pal:

One of the desert's most dreaded citizens paid us a visit today—a big, diamond-back rattlesnake. Dan, Little Beaver, and I were lying on the ground in the cool of the day cat-napping. Happening to look in the direction of one of the pack-saddles, I thought I saw it moving. I rubbed my eyes and looked again. From around the end of it came the snake. And what a snake! It must have been the heavyweight champion of them all. It moved into the open, formed itself into an S, and posed there for many minutes. Then it started towards us slowly, gracefully, rhythmically. Within inches of Little Beaver's bare feet it stopped, raised its head, but without coiling or rattling its tail, and looked us over appraisingly.

Little Beaver and Dan watched the snake with drowsy but calm interest. To them, it was merely another desert friend crossing their trail and pausing to say "Hello!" The inspection of us was thorough. Then, evidently satisfied with its observations and conclusions, it lowered its beady-eyed head, glided around us leisurely, moved down the trail, and disappeared into the desert. Not once did it look back. Not once did it show the least fear. Its confidence in our good will was absolute.

This is country where the dread of snakes, and particularly rattlers, usually maintains panic proportions, except with "originals" like Dan and Little Beaver. They really like snakes, and the bigger the snakes the better they like them. You were not afraid of snakes either, were you! I remember that whenever we encountered one in our back-country travels, you always stood still and poised, and permitted the snake to go about its business undisturbed and unfrightened. As I watched you during those tense moments, it always seemed as though a flash of mutual understanding and respect went from you to the snake, and from the snake to you; like neighbourly radiograms darting between a big dreadnought and a little submarine at sea.

Observant travellers in this part of the country are often astonished to learn that while the poisonous snakes hereabouts seem to take satisfaction in biting White men, they rarely harm the Indians. The snakes have been practising this selective fang-jabbing with marked success for centuries. To most White men the reason for this is incomprehensible. They cannot understand why the snakes should pick on them with such destructive ambitions, and extend immunity to the Indians. Nor is it clear to them how it is that the snakes are able to distinguish so accurately between White men and Red men.

46

Most of the White men who travel or live in this part of the country take the greatest precautions against snakes. They wear high boots, go armed, and are very careful where they place their hands and feet. The Indians do just the reverse. They wear light moccasins or go barefooted, are seldom armed, and pay almost no attention to the snakes. They are perfect targets for fangs, easy ones too, but the snakes prefer to direct their poisonous attentions at the heavily booted, heavily armed White men.

Little Beaver knows why it is that the Indians and the rattlesnakes are on such good terms. So does Dan. And so do I, thanks to my training under your direction. The reason is as simple as it is elemental. But its implications are startling In it, I believe, lie the cause and the remedy for every problem that bothers and baffles humanity today, whether that problem be individual or collective. It may be stated in two words—*mental attitudes*.

The White man has one kind of mental attitude towards snakes; the Indian, an entirely different kind. The White man has been educated to fear snakes, to hate them, and to kill every one he meets. The Indian has been taught to respect and coördinate himself with all forms of animal life. To the Indian the snake is a fellow-creature, a younger brother in the Creation, and so entitled to as much life, liberty, happiness, and consideration as he hopes to enjoy himself. He is not afraid of snakes. He bears them no ill will. He rarely harms them. He attends to his own business, and extends the same privilege to the

47

snakes. As a result there is seldom trouble between them.

Merely a difference in mental attitudes, but often the difference between life and death in results. Strange as it would probably sound to the uninitiated, the snake, with its proverbial wisdom, distinguishes between the mental attitudes of the White man and the Indian, and acts accordingly, returning like for like with interest. The snake strikes the White man's skin body with deadly fury, but what it is really aiming at is the mental malice animating that body. Without the vicious thinking moving it to action, the physical body could not possibly annoy the snake. When the snake strikes, it is attempting to throw its poison against the poison and destruction being projected toward it from the White man's mind and heart.

White men and snakes have been fighting one another in this manner for ages. When a White man and a snake see one another, there is an immediate collision of violently antagonistic thought-forces. The mental impact between them is swift, cruel, and pitiless on both sides. Fear and uncontrolled emotions turn both of them into assassins. The snake meets the White man's unfriendliness with unfriendliness; his ruthlessness with ruthlessness; his venom back of gun, club, or rock with venom back of needle-like fangs. It has been a ceaseless vendetta in which neither White man nor snake has ever really won. And so it will continue, I suppose, until the White man gets the hate and cruelty out of his mind

48

and heart, and learns to appreciate and respect his Creation.

I am grateful to you for helping me understand in a practical way why it is so important for me to keep close watch over my mental attitudes, especially when I happen to be in the vicinity of forms of life supposed to be wild, vicious, destructive, or otherwise bad. I wish I had known about these things years ago. It would have saved me from no end of bites, kicks, stings, slaps, punches, and other unpleasant reactions for which I had been mentally responsible, without being conscious of it.

When you and I went to live together, one of your attendants—a man wise in the inner and outer ways of animals—warned me not to say anything to you with my lips that I did not mean in my heart. I did not have the slightest idea what he was talking about. But then, I did not know that dogs were such natural mind-readers. Humans certainly had to come clean and straight with you, didn't they! I doubt if anyone ever deceived you, at least very much. Or lied to you and got away with it. I never knew you to make a mistake in estimating a human's real inner worth, or lack of it. They could bluff their own kind, but not you.

Humans have a natural capacity for seeing and hearing the mental attitudes in others, but seldom use it. They are inclined to regard it as supernormal, occult, ultra-mysterious, and even dangerous. So they avoid it as much as possible, except perhaps when consulting fortune-tellers.

As a result, humans have acquired the quite general belief that it is possible for them to be one thing on the inside of themselves and something entirely different outside. The notion prevails that as long as one is socially presentable, observes the current conventions, and makes the correct orthodox gestures, he has a right to do as he pleases with his thinking forces. Consequently it is by no means uncommon for a human to give himself an outward veneer of respectability, and then from his withinness cheat, trick, bamboozle, exploit, and maltreat his fellow-beings in ways that no four-legged animal would stoop to use.

If sufficiently stirred in emotions and feelings, this same undisciplined human will hide behind his outward veneer of respectability, and go about injuring and destroying his own kind, with a studied malevolence no jungle animal could even begin to equal. He does not always destroy them physically. He is usually too cowardly for that. He does it mentally. He hacks, slashes, stabs, and lays them low with such deadly concealed weapons as gossip, slander, destructive criticism, envy, hatred, jealousy, suspicion, greed, covetousness, hatred and malice. He is an incipient slayer, stealing about with murder in his heart.

Curiously enough we humans are the only species, as far as I know, that do this. Consequently, we have the dubious distinction of having developed what are probably the only double-faced, double-minded, double-hearted, double-tongued, double-handed, double-dealing, and double-crossing specimens in existence. None of us are really proud of this accomplishment, though, for in our more rational moments—we know that this one human trait alone—malevolent dishonesty—has been responsible for most of our frustration, confusion, friction, failure, discord, strife, misery, hardships, sorrow, want, disease, and war.

But as long as there are desert rats like Dan, and Indians like Little Beaver, and dogs like you, to set us good examples in genuinely and honestly being one's own indiviual self all the way through, there is still hope for the human species.

*I'll be seein' you*

# SISSY

*To*

*Strongheart*
*Eternal Playground*
*Out Yonder*

Dear old Pal:

The desert expedition is over. Dan went in one direction, Little Beaver in another, and I came to this picturesque ranch to spend a few days with that colourful hoss-rassler, Plain Mister Smith. You remember Plain Mister Smith. How could you forget him! How could anyone forget him! He has expanded in many directions since you and I visited him at that little ranch just outside of Hollywood, where he trained and rented horses to the motion-picture studios. Remember those suppers he cooked for us! And the three-way ball games in the corral, when there weren't too many horses inside! And those amusing loafing hours in the barn!

In those days Plain Mister Smith was not very prosperous, but today he is what is known as "in the money." He owns two ranches, one for horses and the other for cattle, is interested in oil and gold on the side, and even threatens to go into politics. But he is a sissy. And you helped to make him one. Perhaps you do not know the meaning of that term. Well, in case you don't, let me say that a sissy is "a male who has womanly traits of character to an inappropriate degree" and is "lacking in manly strength and aggressiveness." I always call him a sissy, just as he calls me every uncomplimentary thing that his imagination can invent. But we do it in a spirit of camaraderie. To have fun. I would not dare call him a sissy in a really offensive way, as he can be plenty tough and rough, with or without guns.

Plain Mister Smith always looks as if he had just stepped out of a Remington painting, with his big Stetson, his vividly colored shirts, his grey, tailored, riding-pants, his red-and-yellow-stitched quarterboots, his jangling silver spurs, and that bowlegged, rolling swagger of his. If his face hadn't come into such frequent and violent contact with fists, bullets, hoofs, and plain old-fashioned prairie earth, he would have been a handsome man of the matinée type. As it is, only his colorful vitality and his clothes save him from being "just a mug." In ordinary city clothes, he would look like something that had been washed in by the tide. But in cowboy clothes and astride a horse, he is, in looks and ability, a buckaroo among the buckaroos.

Plain Mister Smith grew up on the back of a horse. His mother, unable to hire a nurse for him when he was a baby, and being too busy to devote all her time to him, made a soft, open leather bag, tucked her son into it daily, tied him to the saddle on the back of a horse, and let the horse serve as a combination nurse and cradle. As he grew older, he punched cattle from the

Mexican to the Canadian border, and eventually became a top-notch rodeo contestant, competing for money prizes in such events as riding bucking horses and roping, riding, or bulldogging strong-necked steers. Between these engagements he broke and trained horses. His methods were as crude and as cruel as they were spectacular and dangerous. And they were as hard on him as they were on the horse. His favorite procedure was to rope a green horse . . . snub its head to a post . . . tie a heavy handkerchief over its eyes . . . cinch a specially designed bucking saddle on its back . . . force a punishing curb-bit between its teeth . . . and snap the rest of the trick bridle over its head.

Then very carefully he would wedge himself into the saddle. . . . break loose the blindfold and headropes . . . shout at the animal . . . rake its sides with his spurs . . . slap its ears down with his hat . . . perhaps hit it a few times with his short, heavy quirt . . . and then try to ride it "high, wide and handsome." His objective was to stay on that "hurricane deck" and man-handle the horse into a stage of submission. The horses always resisted his interest in them, usually with everything they had. They would charge . . . countercharge . . . stop violently . . . leap, twist, whirl . . . do everything they could think of to get that punishing thing off their backs and free themselves from the pain in their mouths and along their sides and flanks.

Having the better equipment, as well as the advantage, Plain Mister Smith usually won; but not always. Occasionally he would find himself astride a horse that was too "slick" for him, a horse that knew how to outsmart him; and then he was invariably taken to a hospital for repairs. Those "ornery critters," as Plain Mister Smith called them, generally used one of three bucking routines to beat him. They would either start a series of wild, irregular leaps straight up in the air, arching their backs, swinging their rear ends violently left and right, coming down stiff-legged, and jolting him clear out of the saddle. Or they would sideswipe him against some stationary object and knock him out of the saddle. Or— and this was always the most effective—they would rear unexpectedly and throw themselves over backwards on top of him.

On one of his hospital sojourns I went to visit him, and we got to talking about you. He was particularly interested in finding out just what training secrets were used with you to produce such conspicuous success in motion pictures, hoping thereby to learn some new ideas which might be helpful with his horses. I told him there had been no secrets in your training; and that as far as I had been able to observe, your achievements were the result of an amazing bond of coordination and cooperation between you and your teacher and director Larry Trimble. A bond, I emphasized, based on mutual respect . . . mutual affection . . . mutual understanding . . . mutual confidence . . . mutual trust . . . mutual consideration . . . and mutual appreciation.

Plain Mister Smith gasped. He had not expected anything like that. But he was even more surprised when I told him that those associated with you in your educational work never limited you mentally, or otherwise, to being "just a dog"; they treated you as an intelligent fellow-being, with unlimited capacities for independent thinking and activity . . . the exchange of ideas . . . and advancement and accomplishment. He knew that you understood human conversation, and followed direction with intelligent understanding, as he had watched you work in front of the cameras; but it had never occurred to him that this was the result of freeing you from many of the handicaps and restrictions which unenlightened and self-centred human beings have been stupidly clamping down around dogs for centuries.

Plain Mister Smith spent the next several weeks lying in his hospital bed, looking at the ceiling, wondering, and thinking out in new orbits. At the end of this time he had arrived at the following conclusions: (1) that if a dog responded to educational help the way you did, there was nothing to prevent the same thing happening to a horse, or any other animal for that matter; (2) that a horse bucked and kicked because it was filled with fear, and was trying to protect itself; (3) that it would be smarter, and easier on his skeleton, to gentle the fear out of horses, rather than riding and booting it out; (4) that force never got fear out of or real cooperation from anything; and (5) that he would "try a Trimble" on the first horse he got to break, after he got out of the hospital.

I happened to be present at the inauguration of the new method. Plain Mister Smith never does anything by halves. He had picked for the experiment a horse that was supposed to be "plum locoed." Crazy, to you. It was a big, fine-looking animal, but dangerous with body, hoofs, and teeth. And a suicide to ride. Plain Mister Smith slipped into the corral and roped, threw, and hogtied the horse, before it had a chance to attack him. Then he sat on his heels a short distance from its head, and talked to it as one human might talk to another human who was in a state of emotional intoxication. At the end of an hour's talk, he broke loose the ropes and ran for the entrance, with the infuriated animal almost on his heels.

From then on, the ropings and conversations went on mornings and afternoons. Plain Mister Smith made no attempt to touch the horse. In the beginning it was all conversation, pleasant and agreeable talk from a human to a horse. For the first few days the horse strained and struggled to free itself, glaring with eyes almost out of their sockets. Gradually, the fear and the suspicion began to subside. In its place came wonder . . . then curiosity . . . then interest . . . then a timid, shy attempt at friendliness . . . then trust . . . and then confidence. One morning Plain Mister Smith reached over slowly and stroked the animal's neck. There was no resistance. Not even a quiver. In that moment a living entity known as a man, and another living entity known as a horse, broke through the illusion of separateness and found one another.

Plain Mister Smith tried to keep his experiment a secret, but word managed to reach an adjoining ranch that he was breaking the suicide horse, and two cowboys rode over to see the excitement. They walked quietly to the corral, expecting to see Plain Mister Smith and the horse in one of his spectacular rough-riding battles. Instead the horse was lying on its side securely tied; and Plain Mister Smith was seated a short distance away reading to it from a volume of Canadian poems. The cowboys were shocked speechless. Finally one of them recovered sufficiently to cup his hands and yell, "So you've turned Sissy, have you!" And away they ran, and away they rode like gossipy old Paul Reveres, to spread the news.

But this did not deter Plain Mister Smith. He went right on with his experiment. As the weeks went by, he began to discover that the horse, now free from its sense of insecurity, as well as its fear, and its suspicion, and its mistrust, and its timidity, really wanted to be his friend, really wanted to learn . . . and really wanted to co-operate with him. Before the end of the year he had one of the finest stunt horses that ever galloped in front of a motion-picture camera. Understanding and kindness were paying dividends, just as they had with you.

*I'll be seein' you*

# EDUCATORS

*Hollywood*
*California*

*To*

*Strongheart*
*Eternal Playground*
*Out Yonder*

Dear old Pal:

Back in our little house again after some grand adventuring in desert and mountains. For the past week I have been trying to catch up with world news. If I am to believe the newspapers, radio, books, magazines, theatre, motion pictures, and the chatter of my friends, things are in a bad way throughout the human sectors. They are filled with strife, discord, bitterness, hopelessness and despair. Graft, greed, corruption, and violence are rampant. Social, moral, and economic values are topsy-turvy. Apparently no one knows how to be neighbourly. Or wants to be. Friendliness, tolerance, self-respect, and reverence for life appear to be at low ebb. The national and international atmosphere is unwholesome, stupid, lawless, anarchistic, and wanton. In plain words, the world is in a mess.

I dislike having to confess this to a dog, but facts off the end of one's nose are facts off the end of one's nose—aren't they! Some of the two-legged observers of this scene are saying that

59

humanity is at the beginning of a new dark age; that disintegrative forces have so eaten away the foundations of human civilization that it is in grave danger of collapsing and disappearing like other lost civilizations. To which the flippant are replying, "Well, if things are as bad as that, the sooner we crack up the better! Let 'er collapse! We couldn't be any worse off than we are!"

Imagine such things happening to us humans! To us, who consider ourselves so superior to all other forms of organic life. To us, who take such smug pride in our spiritual, mental, and physical attainments! To us, who brag so much of our civilization and accomplishments! Why, we have muddled and complicated everyday life worse than any other species on earth! We have not even mastered the elemental obligation of getting along intelligently with our own kind. We pretend we have. We talk piously about loving our neighbor as ourselves. We harangue one another over the importance of everyone participating constructively in the life of the whole. And then, with a sort of collective wink, we fly at one another's throats and after one another's possessions, with a studied viciousness no other animal could think of.

Everyone agrees that something ought to be done about the situation, and everyone has a remedy, but nearly all of these cure-alls have to do with reforming the other fellow, and the other group, mob, or nation. Apparently no one considers it the least bit important to reform himself, or his own group, mob, or nation first. They must never have heard the ancient precept that to improve one's civilization, one must begin in his own mind, heart, and conduct.

Personally, I do not believe conditions are as serious as they are being reported. The human species is undoubtedly off its social and moral course. The reason? My guess is that we humans have been associating too much with our own species and have turned sour. We have been looking at one another too much, talking with one another too much, milling around with one another too much. We have lost our perspective and our sense of real values. What we need are enriching relationships with, and fresh wisdom from, the animals . . . the birds . . . the insects . . . the reptiles . . . the fish . . . the trees . . . the flowers . . . and all the rest of those neglected neighbors of ours.

I believe it is possible to get the human part of the world back to its original simplicity, goodness, and happiness. But we shall have to go outside the human species to accomplish it. My suggestion would be to put dogs in all our institutions of learning as educators. That is, instead of humans training dogs, let dogs train the humans. I would give every dog, irrespective of age, looks, pedigree, or sex, some kind of a teaching degree like, for instance, "Bachelor of the Art of Felicitous Living" or "Doctor of Good Companioning," and then turn over to them the job of recivilizing and re-educating the human species.

That this has not been tried before is probably due to the prevailing notion that the human has exclusive rights to all knowledge and wisdom, and so needs no help from other forms of life.

Which may explain why we humans are so far behind the "lesser" animals in so many really essential things. My plan would counteract much of this. For one thing, dogs are not only excellent teachers but natural teachers. And they have this advantage over most humans: they can teach by example. Economically, the plan is perfect, as the dog teachers would be no burden on taxpayers. There would be no salaries: teaching equipment would be unnecessary; no buildings would be needed. Their upkeep would be almost nothing, and they would be completely immune from graft and politics.

In this new educational scheme, a dog instructor would be assigned to each human student, and the classroom would be any place the dog and human happened to be. Any part of a mountain would do admirably. But so would a sunny valley, or a stretch of seashore, or a quiet street, or an empty lot, or even an ordinary back yard. The student would be required to wear old clothes, carry a notebook and pencil, and move about with a jaw-gag, which I shall design when I have a little more time. This gag will permit the wearer to inhale air through his mouth, if he cares to, but will prevent words from coming out of his mouth. It will completely shut off all chattering and all giving of orders. This is a very important part of the plan, for being dumb for awhile will tend to sharpen the student's thinking processes, stimulate his powers of imagination, and expand his capacities to receive.

For the curriculum, the dog teacher would be given the freedom of the universe, and the student instructed to trail after him, observing carefully, and setting down in his notebook whatever conclusions he felt were worth setting down. These books would be used later to determine the student's rate of progress, and to estimate his expanding or contracting worth as a citizen of the universe. As part of his examinations, each student would be required to search through a dictionary, or book of synonyms, and compile a list of every meritorious quality he had been able to identify in his dog teacher. That would rock him back on his intellectual heels, wouldn't it! After he had had an opportunity to ponder these qualities, he would be requested to make a list of what he considered his own meritorious qualities, compare them with those of the dog, and write a frank but confidential thesis on which of them was making the better use of his good qualities in the common, everyday things of life.

I shall never forget what happened to my self-esteem when I tried this test with you. I had been wondering which of us was really making the better use of his mental, moral, and physical equipment. I searched all the word-books I had for the names of fine qualities, pausing at each one to see if you made use of it in any way. The results were not only astonishing; they were alarming. I had no idea that you in particular and all dogs in general possessed qualities of such high excellence, or so many of them. I wondered how I could have looked at dogs for so many years without having noticed these qualities before. Next, I wrote down in a generous way what I believed to be all my own good qualities.

Then the shock! The terrible shock! I compared our lists. I will tell you the truth! Your qualities and your undeviating loyalty to them at all times, in all places, and under all circumstances sent me and my list into an almost complete eclipse. I had been bested by a dog, but I had learned something about myself and life that I sadly needed to know.

That is why I am such a booster for dogs as educators. Not any special type of dog, but all dogs. Most intelligent men and women agree that you dogs have unusual capacities for taking the friction, and the frustration, and the futility out of human beings. They also agree that every human is a better citizen through associating with a dog. My scheme would simply extend this fine, constructive work. And besides, it is high time that you dogs had a turn at this teaching activity. My species has been at it too long. We are taught out. Look where we have bogged you dogs, for instance! After centuries of close association with you, we have taught you—what? To be subordinate pets . . . hunters . . . fighters . . . exhibitionists . . . personal and enslaved servitors. We have done almost nothing to really understand you, or to help you expand to the state of being and usefulness of which all of you are capable.

What a magnificent educator you were! And still are! You may have been without academic knowledge. You may have lacked the things the average human believes make up a liberal education. And you may have been "only a dog" and "a dumb thing." But you influenced for

64

the better every human who came within your radius, even the radius of your photograph. You taught people without being conscious of it. You took the tension out of them. Broadened and deepened their minds and hearts. Helped them to achieve better levels of themselves. Revitalized them. Inspired them. Showed them how to stretch out to their finer energies. Lured them into being more simple, more natural, happier, freer, and more divinely irresponsible. Encouraged them to live and to love more abundantly. You satisfied, in a degree, their hunger for the Infinite.

That, and more, you did through the irresistible magic of your fine example. And if that isn't good educational work, what is it?

*I'll be seein' you*

## DOGFISH

*Pacific Ocean*

*To*

*Strongheart*
*Eternal Playground*
*Out Yonder*

Dear old Pal:

I am heading West for the East, riding on a big luxury liner, bound on a trip around the world. Several decks below where I am sunbathing is the Pacific Ocean in one of its most pacific moods. There isn't even a ripple on the water as far as the eye can see. San Francisco is three days astern, Yokohama nine days ahead. Seagoing life thus far has been a matter of following the lines of least resistance under ideal conditions. We eat frequently, play games that do not require too much effort, read, doze, sleep, and in the cool of the day spread ourselves and strut up and down the promenade deck.

The only discordant note in this lazy routine was a bon voyage book that a friend gave me to read. It was a book about dogs, and included a photograph of you. By the way, do you remember all those dog books I tried to read to you? You would listen politely for several pages, then yawn, roll over, and go to sleep. Somehow or other I could never get you interested in books about dogs. They always bored you into slumberland.

66

And I think I know why. You found them too full of human sense and too lacking in dog sense. Well, I don't blame you. You didn't care for fiction either; but this I attributed to your lack of interest in the humans' rather loose, all-the-year-round, open mating season, and your indifference to the over-emphasis they placed on sex.

Biography was also tedious for you. Was that because you did not think the writers knew very much about real living, as you understood the meaning of that term? I wonder! But you did like poetry with substance and a tang to it . . . and children's stories . . . and fairy tales . . . and essays from purified-heart sources. At least you never yawned or went to sleep while I was reading them to you.

The bon voyage book which I read today has irked me to my very heels. It was a reheated goulash of all the unintelligent, stupid, and hackneyed things that human beings have been saying about dogs, since the first time they began making mistakes about them. The author introduced himself as one of the greatest authorities in the world on breeding, training, and exhibiting dogs, especially police dogs. He had what is known as an authority complex, and all through the book he had it spread out and up like a peacock's tail. He did not write opinions about dogs; he handed down irrevocable decisions about them.

He would name a certain breed, and then in substance say this, "Note carefully the circle I have drawn around this type of dog. This is the extent of their capacity for accomplishment. Within these boundaries these dogs can be

67

trained, by using my methods or having me do it for you at so-much by the week, to perform thus and so. No more, no less. Beyond these defined limits these dogs can never go, now or ever."

I wanted to put the war tones into my voice, fling it across space, and say to that self-nominated, self-elected expert, wherever he was, "Listen, you! Why shouldn't dogs go beyond those narrow, shallow, silly limits of yours? Where do you get the right to circumscribe or restrict any form of life in God's boundless creation? Who gave you permission to say to any form of life, 'Thus far and no farther'? Has the Creator gone on a vacation and turned the earth over to you to manage? Are you taking the Creator's place? Substituting for Him? Acting as His stand-in? If not, what entitles you to speak with such finality? Have you risen high enough in the scale of being . . . have you acquired enough Cosmic wisdom and experience . . . have you perfected your own life sufficiently, for such a transcendent job?" He would probably bark out an emphatic "Yes!" and that would leave me right where I started.

He wrote his own biography in his chapter on the training of dogs. He is a throw-back from those dark ages in human experience when blustering vanity went hand-in-hand with inconsiderate, unrestrained force. The era of "red-blooded, two-fisted, he-men." He belongs to that rapidly dwindling school of dog-handlers which goes in extensively for autocratic, heavy-handed, mechanical training with its accompanying harsh commands, equally harsh domination, and severe discipline. He believes in intimidation and force.

68

But then, he regards dogs as material objects, without much intelligence, and entirely without individual rights.

He devoted a number of pages to you and your accomplishments, but he did not attempt to put any borders around you, probably because your success was too well established. He spoke of you as a most unusual dog, but back of the compliment was the implication that you were so unusual that you could almost be classified as a freak. He made no effort to explain how it was that you were able to do so many, many things beyond the boundaries he had officially set for dogs in general and your breed in particular. I do not believe he could have explained you. I doubt if he had enough mental horsepower to take him up to where you "lived, moved, and had your being."

I wonder what he would think, if he knew that those associated with you had spent most of their time trying to free you from the kind of limitations he was clamping down on dogs in almost every sentence he wrote! I wonder what he would say, if he knew that those close to you had never thought of you or spoken to you as "just a dog"; but, instead, had given you full recognition as a rational unit in the universe . . . with unlimited potentialities for independent thought . . . understanding . . . reasoning . . . the exchange of ideas . . . response and cooperation . . . expression . . . achievement . . . and with just as important rights in the world as the human!

Had he known some of these things, he would never have written that book about dogs. Nor would he ever again recommend or use force in

F

the training of an animal. For he would know, not theoretically but in a demonstrable way, that coordination or cooperation between any and all forms of organic life is successful only when it is founded on mutual respect . . . mutual understanding . . . and mutual love. He made the quite common mistake of passing along the opinions of others without having reasoned them out. Consequently, he did not seem to know that something mental and enduring back of his own physical appearance, and something equally mental and equally enduring back of every dog's physical appearance, were inseparably interrelated in the great Oneness of life. One day he will find this astonishing trail, and then he will probably stop training dogs for awhile, and let them train him.

When I finished the book I walked up and down one of the lower decks, wondering what I ought to do with it. Ordinarily, I like to share books with others. But not this one. Glancing over the rail I had my answer. Swimming along with the ship was a school of dogfish. *Dog*fish! if you please. What a symbolical opportunity! They were not fussy about their literature, I knew. So I heaved the book at the leading fish with the compliments of both of us. My intent was better than my aim, my timing, or my execution. I did not realize that the ship and the fish were travelling so fast. The book opened in the middle, banked itself momentarily against the wind like a fantastic bird out of a fairy story that had forgotten to bring its head and tail along, and then plopped on top of the water just back of the last fish.

Instantly the ocean became a whirlpool at that particular spot. The dogfish had reversed themselves at full speed. It was an astounding maneuver. There was a flashing of sleek, dark bodies, and rows of wicked-looking white teeth. Every fish appeared to lunge and snap at the book at the same time. The water seethed with fury and foam. Then there was a sudden calm. No dogfish! No dog book!

*I'll be seein' you*

# MUCH TOO MUCHNESS

*Pacific Ocean*

*To*
*Strongheart*
*Eternal Playground*
*Out Yonder*

Dear old Pal:

Our ship paused at Honolulu yesterday. Honolulu is a colorful and very gay city on the glamorous island of Oahu, where the inhabitants practice such seductive enchantments that visitors usually lose all desire either to proceed on their journeys or return home. This sorcery was apparent the moment the ship slowed down outside the harbor. Up the gangway came boatloads of Islanders with laughing faces . . . high enthusiasm . . . warm words of welcome . . . string instruments . . . songs . . . heavily perfumed flower leis . . . and the freedom of all the Islands.

The ship was to be in port ten hours. "Perfect!" said Island friends. "Everything is arranged. In ten hours you are going to see what ordinarily takes ten weeks!"

Nine hours and fifty-eight minutes later I was back aboard the ship, so overstuffed with sights, impressions, information, and rich food that I waddled both mentally and physically. It had been like a fantastic dream. Or like watching the universe from the front seat of a well-greased roller coaster. We moved at top speed in auto-mobiles, boats, and airplanes. Mountains, valleys, waterfalls, parks, buildings, houses, golf courses, polo fields, plantations, ships, and people flashed in and out of vision as though they were parts of a hastily assembled but still unedited movie scenic. At frequent intervals, we stopped long enough to shake hands with men and women and have refreshments. Not caring for alcoholic beverages, I devoted my efforts to the food in a big way.

Back aboard the ship again, I leaned sluggishly against the ship's rail and watched native boys dive for money from the various decks, and listened to the Islanders on the pier sing their hauntingly lovely alohas. Then I went below. Kato, my diminutive cabin boy, who has been taking a grandmotherly interest in me since we left the United States, was standing at the door of my room waiting for me. His customary smile was missing, and he was shaking his head disap-provingly. Something was wrong. I went into the room and threw myself exhaustedly into a chair.

Kato followed me in. For a moment he stared at me from an expressionless face. Then he said: "No good! Much too muchness!"

"Much too what?" I asked.

He pointed at my head. Then at my stomach. Then he whirled his hand violently in various directions—to illustrate me in action, I suppose. "Much too muchness!" he replied. "Go too much! See too much! Eat too much! Bad! Very bad!" Following which he shrugged his shoulders, stooped and picked up a pair of shoes that needed cleaning, and marched out of the room. I was in disgrace. And here is the real reason for it. Long before we reached Honolulu, I asked Kato, who is quite an expert in matters of this kind, what I should do when I went ashore to get the real flavor of the Island. He spent hours working out an itinerary for me.

Yesterday morning he selected and brought to me an unusually substantial breakfast, and advised me not to eat again until I returned to the ship, at which time, he said, he would have a special Hawaiian dinner for me. I did not follow his itinerary, and I did not follow his instructions about not eating. As a matter of fact I over-ate to such a degree that I was unable to eat any of the dinner he had spent all day arranging for me.

Why do you suppose it is that humans overdo things the way I did yesterday? And if you can answer that one, then tell me how it is that dogs maintain such temperate habits and good sense in their physical activities in general, and in their eating and drinking in particular? No dog would have eaten as much unneeded food as I did yesterday. You never overate, did you! Even when your plate was piled high with food you particularly liked. You satisfied your hunger. You never fed appetite. I remember, too, that at least every other week you went an entire day without food, and gave your digestive apparatus a rest. Where did you learn to do that? Kato does the same thing. He says that occasional fasting makes his head feel happy, and puts bounce into his body.

My problem at the moment is how I can square

myself with Kato. He has been teaching me new ways to broaden my mental, spiritual, and esthetic horizons; and I do not want to have it interrupted. Mind you, he does not know he is teaching me. I am, in a way, sneaking it. He goes about his day's job devotedly, happily, filled with good intentions, and I watch him surreptitiously, and learn how to do better with my own life. His job is a humble one. He cleans rooms, presses clothes, shines shoes, waits on table, helps wash dishes, assists in the laundry, runs errands, and does odd jobs. He works long hours for very little pay. When they need his kind, they usually order them by the wholesale and list them by numbers instead of by names.

Nevertheless, and I say this with the pride of discovery, Kato is one of the finest gentlemen I have ever met, on land or at sea. Now a gentleman, it is generally agreed, is the full fragrant flowering of the genus *Homo*, irrespective of type, coloring, occupation, or social standing. He is supposed to have a pleasing personal appearance . . . agreeable manners . . . a modulated voice . . . qualities valuable to society . . . self-confidence . . . consistent regard for moral standards . . . respect for himself . . . respect for others . . . wholesome inclinations . . . self-control . . . an affirmative attitude towards life . . . enthusiasm . . . a sense of humor . . . the desire to share . . . and enough mental poise to make him immune to insult, bitterness, retaliation, or revenge.

In his thinking, and in his living, and in his speaking, the gentleman is supposed to be kind . . . tolerant . . . generous . . . considerate . .

75

honest . . . adaptable . . . a good neighbor . . .
loyal to his private ideals . . . childlike in his
willingness to learn; and free from all sense of
inferiority, whatever his position and circumstances . . . all narrow class interests . . . all
secret impurities . . . prejudices . . . greed . . .
pretense . . . gossip . . . slander . . . condemnation
. . . destructive criticism . . . and the ambition to
control and manipulate the lives of others.

That is the blueprint of a gentleman. And
again I say that Kato is one of the finest gentlemen I have ever met, on land or at sea. Kato
never seems to regret that life is not something
else. Like you dogs, he takes life as he finds it
and makes it yield him rich dividends in happiness. As far as I have been able to observe, he
never permits everyday existence to become
"wearisome, stale, flat and unprofitable," although
from surface appearances he has every right to.
He lifts commonplace drudgery, like the scrubbing
of floors and bathtubs, into rhythmic artistry.
His desire to share . . . to please . . . and to be
helpful begins so deep down inside him that when
it flows out into action, it glorifies everything
he does.

(*Later*) I have thought of a plan to get myself
back into Kato's good graces. Within the next
hour he will have to bring the dinner menu.
When he comes I shall make profuse apologies
for my conduct yesterday. I shall tell him that
much too muchness is not an Occidental in-
discretion, as he may have been believing, but an
Occidental disease, which hits us without warning, and makes us act like—well, like Occidentals.

Then I shall ask him to order my dinner, without even looking at the menu.

Whatever comes of it, though, Kato is always going to be a sparkling and glowing memory in my collection. Not only that, but Japan is going to be a finer and fairer nation, just because I have been privileged to know that humble little Japanese, and watch him do lowly, humdrum things sublimely. He does not know it, but he has made me a better citizen of the universe by just being himself—all the way through.

*I'll be seein' you*

## SHIPMATES

*Pacific Ocean*

*To*
*Strongheart*
*Eternal Playground*
*Out Yonder*

Dear old Pal:

Japan is just over a watery horizon line and because of that fact the passengers are going through a disintegrating process of relationships peculiar to the human species. Up until last night we were like a big, happy family aboard this ship—one for all and all for one. This morning, however, men and women are moving about the decks with a formality that is chilling the very atmosphere. When we first came aboard at San Francisco everyone laid aside his national, religious, political, and social identities. With them went most of the accompanying prejudices, too. Then almost without effort we blended into a oneness of interest and action. Now we are disentangling ourselves from one another, and resuming our individual pride in race, place, and face.

For inconsistency in relationships we humans are probably the all-species champions. We make them when they serve our purposes, and we break them when they don't. The more pessimistic critics among us are openly declaring that we are not only losing the real meaning of relationships, but even the ability to live with one another in a sensible, neighborly way. They say that while we know most of the theories about these things, we lack the disciplined intelligence to make them work. Perhaps this is true. But I do know that it is possible for humans to make group relationships flexible, charming, and satisfactory. It has been demonstrated continuously during our present voyage across the Pacific.

For a week and a half, a variegated assortment of us from many different countries, with different educational backgrounds, and widely differing political, social and religious views, have been living closely together aboard this ship, and maintaining almost flawless relationships with one another. So, you see, we can do it when we have a mind to. And how do you suppose we made it work? With dog fundamentals! We used dog fundamentals! No worries. No responsibilities. No yesterdays or tomorrows. No competitive action. No exploitation of one another. No struggling after material things. Instead, enthusiastic identification with one another.

We wanted to be happy. But what was more important, we wanted others to be happy with us. And so we were happy. Very happy. We stopped trying to run the universe. Stopped trying to manage the lives of others. Instead we used the dog technique of taking whatever happened and turning it into amusing adventure. We dared to step out of our conventional ceremonial routines and be gay and frolicsome. We dared take off some of our clamps and be more of our real selves. We looked for the good in others. And actually found it. We took the emphasis off "yours" and "mine" and put it on "ours." Then we uncorked our childhearts, turned the ship into a floating playground, and had fun—simple, natural, spontaneous, invigorating, wholesome fun.

The end came abruptly last night when a serpent got into our happy Eden. A radio-serpent! And it coiled, rattled its tail, and hissed and spat news flashes at us! Hot news flashes! News flashes that knocked our seagoing family apart like well-hit bowling-pins! And what a barrage! War . . . crime . . . lawlessness . . . injustice . . . corruption . . . cruelty . . . suffering . . . commercial banditry . . . ruthless disregard for life . . . organized ignorance lock-stepping the highways and bellowing for attention . . . political, religious, and business opportunists regimenting willing minds and bodies and snapping whips over them . . . men and women spoiled by fame and fortune behaving like defective children, and receiving the plaudits of millions . . . crafty, self-interested manipulators inflaming nation against nation, class against class, and man against man.

And all this, mind you, coming from parts of the world supposed to be in advanced states of intellectual, ethical, and social development. They really sounded more like undercover reports from regions of abysmal darkness and depravity; regions into which religion and education had never been able to penetrate. And almost every item was justifying the charge so frequently made, that while humans occasionally talk like gentlemen and scholars, they invariably act like fools. I was really ashamed of my own species. It seemed incredible that anyone could do the things many of them were doing.

Instead of bringing us the kind of news that would have heartened us, made us proud of our kind, and brought us closer together in a common purpose, that radio-serpent was flinging at us stories of individual and group imperfections; of humanity's growing disunity; of its animosities and antagonisms. It was drumming up and glorifying the ancient mesmeric jungle error that, in order to exist, the individual and his particular pack must fight all the others; must possess or be possessed; must conquer or be conquered; must kill and destroy or be killed and destroyed.

By the time the broadcast was over we had all been reminded in a very definite way that the time had arrived for us to unscramble ourselves socially and materially, and return to our absurd little earth groupings, with their equally absurd gradations and labels. We had come out of our pigeon-holes for awhile, and now we are about to go back into them again. Silly, isn't it! The reason for this? Well, I am told that most of it comes from the human's backwardness in learning that he is part of a continuing, universal plan and purpose, rather than a detached little two-legged item riding around rather desperately on a spinning, material earth, with almost everything trying to knock him off it. The clearer-visioned among us, however, those who have grasped something of eternal Truth, are able to get glorious

81

glimpses of the coördination and coöperation forever going on between the Creator, the Created, and the Creation. But that takes spiritual altitude.

Trying to understand his place and relationship obligations in the universe is usually difficult for the human. But, then, the human has a habit of looking at life along low and rather misty earth levels. He is like one peering through a camera lens that is out of focus and seeing magnified distortions of a beautiful landscape. If he accepts the distortions as true he is apt to be confused and discouraged with the outlook. Assuming, in the same sense, that all the out-of-focus things his material senses report are true, he comes to regard life as a limited, precarious arrangement, in which everything is in conflict with everything else. That makes him fearful about his own safety, and out of that disturbing emotion shoot practically all of his antisocial inclinations and practices.

Trying to get the human to understand that life is not an arena, but a Fellowship of infinite proportions, is a problem that has been engaging the attention of educational leaders for centuries. They have made considerable headway, but we are still confronted by the embarrassing fact of being unable to live happily and intelligently with one another with any great degree of success. Some even go as far as to say that we are actually trailing back of most of the other animals, the birds, the insects, the reptiles, and even the fishes, in these matters. What we humans should do, between you and me, is to set aside our pride, step out of our exclusiveness and snootiness, and borrow some fresh and workable ideas about life and relationships from you dogs. It would be a long stoop for our haughty backs but, I will guarantee, an elevating one. Imagine what could happen to the world, for instance, if within the next hour every man, woman, and child began practicing the sparkling dog method of regarding life as an adventure to be met, experienced, and shared together!

*I'll be seein' you*

*ADEPTS*

                                          *Tokio*
                                          *Japan*

*To*

*Strongheart*
*Eternal Playground*
*Out Yonder*

Dear old Pal:

As a fitting climax to weeks of exploring the highways and byways of Japan, I attended a tea-ceremony today. Now don't start getting bored. It was a tea-ceremony, not a tea-party. I remember what a burden it was for you to have to watch humans sip tea and chatter about themselves and others. But this was different; very, very different. A tea-ceremony is one of the most important and impressive historical rituals in the life of the Japanese people. It is an esthetic communion service. A service in which worldly values are set aside, and minds and hearts consecrated to search for the beautiful, the good, the true, and the eternal.

Through inner purification the tea-cultists learn how to spiritualize their thinking and then move from form to symbolism, and from symbolism into the boundless realm of ideas. In this realm they develop such keen powers of discernment, that they are able to find beauty and inspiration in things that most humans would consider ugly and repellent. They learn to take the physically incomplete, and complete it spiritually; to take the physically imperfect, and perfect it in the same way. They drink tea, of course, but that is almost a minor part of the ceremony. The real objective is to clear the inner vision, and experience the greater Loveliness back of the loveliness fashioned by Nature and the hand of man. Thus they seek to move outward and upward towards the eternal Source of all perfection.

Our Tea-master today was a man much honored in Japan for his wisdom, his services to cultural education, and his efforts to preserve the best in his country's traditions. My companion and interpreter was a philosophical little Japanese Statesman who, while small of body, was a giant in his wisdom, sympathies, enthusiasms, and kindly humor. When we reached the gate to the estate where the ceremony was to take place, the little Statesman took off his silk hat, mopped his brow, and whispered, "Appreciation with discernment is the secret gateway to the abounding life." Then he knocked with his gold-headed cane.

The gate opened instantly. Just inside, standing in the middle of the path, was the Tea-master. He was completely bald, had one of the kindest faces I have ever seen, and was wearing a simple black kimono. Back of him stood his assistant and four student-guests. The ceremonial bowing lasted for many minutes. Then with the Tea-master leading the way, we walked slowly through the large formal gardens—an unforgettable experience. Every few feet we paused to admire and praise the arrangements of flowers, trees, rocks, miniature waterfalls, ponds, and bridges. This was all part of the ceremony. Everything in the gardens had been placed in its respective position as a symbol. Our part was to hunt for the meanings, in preparation for what was to follow.

The tea-house, a rare example of ancient Japanese architecture, was tucked away in a grove of enormous pine trees. Just before reaching it we stopped to let water from a long bamboo pipe wet our hands as a gesture of our desire to purify ourselves. The entrance into the tea-house was so low that everyone had to bend almost double to get inside. This to remind us of the need for humility. The interior consisted of a single room in natural pine. In a shallow alcove hung a hand-painted classical poem on a scroll, and below it a blue vase with a single white flower. On the pine posts about the room were carved the names of generations of masters who had prepared tea there. The almost complete absence of decorations was due to the Japanese conviction that severe simplicity is best conducive to introspection and meditation.

The Tea-master knelt before a black, gold-lacquered chest in which were his powdered tea, copper kettles, bowls, incense burners, and other utensils. The assistant knelt at his side. We guests formed a half-circle back of them, the Japanese kneeling, and I sitting cross-legged by special dispensation. The preparation of the individual bowls of tea was like watching a fine old Japanese color print in slow motion. The precision and rhythm of it were worth crossing an ocean to watch. Every move the Tea-master made was an almost exact duplicate of the moves that every master has made at tea-ceremonies, since they were inaugurated in the dim long-ago by Buddhist monks as a means of worshipping refinement and purity.

As each bowl of tea was prepared the assistant would move ceremoniously across the highly polished floor on his knees and present it to one of us. The tea was sipped slowly to the accompaniment of soft-spoken conversation. Then the exquisitely designed and priceless tea utensils were reverently passed from hand to hand for detailed examination. This was one of the most significant parts of the ceremony. We were, I learned, paying homage not only to the inspired artists who fashioned the tea-things, but also to the vast, unbroken chain of known and unknown fellow-beings in all centuries who, having walked the earth for awhile, tried to make it better, lovelier, happier, or holier as they went along their journeys.

As the little Statesman expressed it, we were seeking through inner refinement, humility, teach-ableness, and concentration on loveliness, to attain fullness of observation. Seeking through fullness of observation, to experience revelation. And seeking through revelation, to arrive at the fullness of understanding.

In the cool of the day we all went into the

gardens again, each to follow his own inner urge. The Tea-master, the little Statesman, and I wandered around for awhile and then found an old stone bench, where we had marvelous views of the surrounding country. All about the grounds were students of the master. They had come from all parts of the nation to learn the traditional Japanese art of living with grace and charm. Some of them were motionless in quiet meditation, others walking slowly along flower-lined paths. Their courses consist of the cultivation of wisdom, tranquility, poise and courtesy, etiquette, architecture, landscape gardening, flower arrangement, painting, interior decorating, poetry, music, the practice of good conduct, and the broadening and deepening of discriminating appreciation.

I asked the Tea-master how one could find the greatest satisfaction in life. He thought for some moments and then said gently, via the little Statesman, "By disciplining one's self, and learning to live divinely in small as well as great things." I asked him if he thought it possible to live divinely in a world so filled with hatred and violence. There was a whispered consultation, then both of them nodded their heads vigorously. They had no doubts about it. "It is not a matter of choice," said the Tea-master. "We must either live divinely or go through corrective and cleansing processes until we do so. In this each of us is responsible only for himself."

I asked them if they would tell me some of the qualities they considered requisite for living what they called "the superior life." Again there was a whispered consultation. Then they

88

began naming qualities. Listen to them: love
. . . contentment . . . unselfishness . . . appreciation . . . loyalty . . . sincerity . . . devotion . . .
enthusiasm . . . joy . . . simplicity . . . frugality
. . . gratitude . . . self-control . . . faith . . . kindness . . . the capacity for small enjoyments . . .
serenity . . . honesty . . . poise . . . genuineness
. . . courage . . . sympathy . . . tolerance . . .
understanding . . . good manners . . . strong
observation . . . strength with gentleness . . . unselfish attitudes . . . dignity . . . freedom from
evil purposes . . . and the ability to be interested
in people and things for their own sakes and not
for personal return.

"Suppose one had all these qualities," I said
to the little Statesman. "And suppose he lived
them so silently, modestly, but radiantly, that
men, women, and children—no matter what
language they spoke—were happier and better
for even a glimpse of him walking down the
street. What would you call one like that here in
the Orient? "

There was much animated conversation in
Japanese. Then the little Statesman answered,
"He would be one of the enlightened ones," he
said. "We would call him an adept, or a master.
We would both be honored to sit at the feet of
such a one and learn from him." For awhile we
sat in silence, looking out across the gardens.
Then the little Statesman, who had evidently
been giving the matter considerable thought,
turned and asked me if I had ever met such a
one in my travels. I nodded.

"An American?" he queried, enthusiastically.

"Only by adoption," I told him. "His name is Strongheart."

"An Indian!" he exclaimed like a puzzled child.

"No," I said, "most people call him a dog."

*I'll be seein' you*

# MONKEYS

Nikko
Japan

To

*Strongheart*
*Eternal Playground*
*Out Yonder*

Dear old Pal:

I am at Nikko, and Nikko is an unbelievably lovely temple town in the mountains about four hours by train from Tokio. The Japanese say of it, "Never say Kikko (magnificent) until you have seen Nikko." The entire district is breath-taking in its splendor. No one, according to the legends, ever leaves here disappointed, except with himself. Most of the temples and shrines are in the midst of giant cryptomeria trees. The gorgeousness of their architecture and coloring baffles description. You would not care for them, though, as the temple steps are narrow and steep, and the floors inside very slippery; but you would love the district. It was made to order for a dog like you. There are towering mountains to climb, great waterfalls to play with, all kinds of lakes and rivers to swim in, and lots of unusual places in which to hunt for adventure. You would like the people, too. They are gentle in manners and speech, and very friendly. Humans apparently do not wear bayonets on their thinking in these holy mountains.

I climbed one of the tall mountains this morning, moving over trails worn deep by generations of bare feet. Coming down by a different route, I found myself in the precincts of one of the large temples, and wandered about in it for hours marveling at the beauty wrought by inspired and consecrated imaginations and hands.

Eventually I found myself in front of a sacred stable, sacred because various emperors had kept therein their riding-horses. One was in there as I looked, eating food presents brought to him by pilgrims. He was a highly venerated horse, but I noticed he had to flick flies off himself with his tail just like an ordinary nag.

Happening to glance over the stable door, I saw something that startled me more than anything I have seen since leaving home. Three little carved monkeys sitting in a panel of rich green, gold, and blue foliage! The first had his hands over his eyes, the second over his ears, and the third over his mouth; illustrating the ancient precept, to see no evil, hear no evil, and speak no evil. Three of my most cherished and admired friends! And there they were over a stable door! In reproduced forms these little monkeys have been going into homes all over the world for centuries, carrying on their subtle but effective missionary work, of persuading humans to be more thoughtful and considerate in their dealings with their fellow-beings. You may remember the trio I had on the table by the bed in our sleeping-room. You should, you sniffed at them enough. I never knew before where they originated.

Long, long ago the monkeys were cut out of a block of wood by a left-handed woodcarver named Hidari Jingoro. Remember that name, for if you two ever cross trails out there in the Eternal Playground, you will have much to share with one another. Both of you have the kind of qualities that always make for great and enduring friendship: vitality of being . . . enthusiasm . . . spontaneity . . . naturalness . . . happiness . . . understanding . . . sincerity . . . honesty . . . adaptability . . . appreciation . . . unselfishness . . . gratitude . . . courage . . . sympathy . . . detached attachments . . . real humility . . . breadth of heart . . . and love which "thinketh no evil."

Like you, Jingoro moved through his earth life clear-eyed, in full stride, and unafraid. Like you, he took life as he found it, and making it worth while for others made it worth while for himself. Like you, he always lived at his circumference. Like you, he possessed the capacity to use and enjoy the things he had. It is not surprising then that he should have become one of the great artists of all time. They say of him that he put his whole mind and heart into everything he did. But it is apparent that he first put enduring values into his mind and heart.

Jingoro was not ambitious for fame, wealth, power, or even social approval. Instead he sought to forget himself in the service of the supreme Artist, to be an instrument for that eternal beauty which exceeds time and finiteness. His quest was for the divine. He hunted for it everywhere, searched for it in everything; and particularly in Nature, animals, birds, and insects.

Finding these divine imprints, he would translate them through the medium of sculpture, a language all humans could understand. An eloquent language, too; for any human can stand in front of a Jingoro carving and, provided he is receptive enough, hear that wise, kindly philosopher speaking eternal verities across the ages; can hear him saying simple, amusing, profound things that are good for men and women to know and practice.

Hidari Jingoro was a superlative man. And he still is, even though Public Opinion insists upon classifying him as dead and buried, and his usefulness forever ended. Like you. If it were possible to sit down with Public Opinion as one might with a human, I should like to say to it something like this, "If, as you insist, Mister Public Opinion, Jingoro is dead, do you consider him to be dead all over? That is, did all of him die and pass away, or only part of him? If only part of him died, what happened to the rest of him? And what is that 'rest of him' doing now?"

Mister Public Opinion would undoubtedly fix a hard, suspicious eye on me and reply, "Now don't be silly! Of course Jingoro is dead. Everyone knows that. And he's dead all over, except perhaps for whatever soul part of him may have escaped to some more spiritual state of existence. But as far as you and I are concerned he is definitely and thoroughly dead."

To back this up, Mister Public Opinion would probably point out that no one could produce Jingoro's skeleton-and-skin body, by which people identified him in these mountains centuries ago, and inside of which he was supposed to live. If available, Mister Public Opinion would also show me documents to prove that at a certain hour, on a certain day, of a certain year, Jingoro's physical body stopped functioning; that it had been pronounced lifeless by duly constituted authorities; that it had been buried in the ground; and had since returned to its native elements and disappeared. Which, as far as Mister Public Opinion is concerned, would have completed a perfect case.

"But what about all this sculpture?" I would ask. "What about all the exquisite carvings that his understanding mind, his sympathetic heart, and his sensitive hands brought into human visibility? They are still here with us. And are they not just as much a part of his being now, as they were when he was alive according to your definitions of aliveness? Are they not just as vital and vibrant with his wisdom, his eloquence, his skill, his gayety, his charm, and his emotional, esthetic, and spiritual uplift, as they were when he first exhibited them in the long ago?

"You say that all of him is dead. But what about the mental and spiritual part of him? What about his qualities; those inner assets of his, which gave him his distinct individuality and flavoring, animated him, lifted him to such artistic and moral elevation, distinguished him from all other men, and made him 'one of earth's immortals'? Jingoro had qualities of exceptional excellence. All the world knows that. But what happened to them? Qualities like that cannot disintegrate and die. Or be buried in a hole in the ground. They are not made of that kind of substance. They belonged, and still belong, to an infinite, eternal, and forever-continuing order of things. They are deathless. And that would make Jingoro just as deathless, and just as enduring, as his qualities, wouldn't it?"

As a matter of fact, Strongheart, if it came to a show-down, it might be discovered that at this very moment in history, Jingoro is more alive, more useful, and more influential without a skin-and-bone body than most present-day citizens of the earth are with them. Shocking? Not at all, except in the sense that humans in the mass are so backward in discovering that their material senses report but an infinitesimal fraction of man's true dimensions; and almost nothing of his real height, depth, breadth, scope, capacity, importance, grandeur, and purpose.

We humans are all more or less crawling around in the mesmeric illusion that man is a fragile, organic entity bounded by skin dimensions, and that life is an uncertain force inside this skin body, animating it through a bewildering routine of birth, growth, maturity, decay, and death. And we insist upon believing this in spite of the counsel of generations of clear-visioned, spiritual Teachers that man (the real man) is here and now the "image," "likeness," and "expression," or pressing-out, of God; and so of necessity a mental, divine, boundless, eternal being; an individual consciousness; as perfect in a degree as his Maker; and forever needed to complete the allness of Creation.

But we are doing better, let me add. We are not trying as hard as we did to contract the Infinite and make it fit into our little finite plans and ambitions. Instead we are learning, slowly, perhaps, but surely how to adjust ourselves to the Infinite and move in rhythm with it. And would you like to know where we have been getting much of our inspiration for this? From luminous fellow-beings like you and Jingoro. Luminous fellows who, rising above species, nationality, group, classification, definition, and even materiality, lived, loved, and shared abundantly, and through their fine examples gave the rest of us good compass directions by which we could the better steer our own lives.

*I'll be seein' you*

## MOUNTS OF VISION

*Mount Hiei*
*Japan*

*To*

*Strongheart*
*Eternal Playground*
*Out Yonder*

Dear old Pal:

Since early morning I have been exploring one of Japan's sacred mountains with a stout-legged, smiling, universally minded Buddhist priest. He lives in a copper-roofed monastery of red and gold lacquer, and spends most of his spare time climbing mountains and listening to what Nature has to teach him. At the moment I am sitting on a cliff looking down upon one of Japan's most cherished views. It is late afternoon and everything is drenched in the colors of a gaudy, theatrical sunset. Below me to the left is Lake Biwar, the largest body of fresh water in the kingdom. To the right, the ancient city of Kyoto. In the background, a billowy sea of fantastically tinted mountains. It is the priest's favorite spot for observation and meditation.

Just back of me is a forest of great cedar and cypress trees in which dusk is fast gathering. Out of its mystery come the voices of priests chanting and making ceremonial calls from station to station around the temples. Blending with it is the smell of earth and growing things, and the pungent fragrance of incense. The stout-legged priest is in there contributing his part to it all. In his temple, prayers are offered day and night without interruption for the health and long life of the Imperial family, and the prosperity of the nation.

You would approve of this place. It has the things you are so fond of—height, distance, fragrant air, solitude, stillness, and a feeling of good purpose everywhere. Your liking for climbing to high places and looking off always interested and puzzled me. Whenever it was your turn to lead our little expeditions afield, you always headed for an elevation, didn't you! A mountain top, if one were available; if not, then the top of a hill with as few humans on it as possible. Reaching your objective, you invariably made yourself comfortable and stared off towards distant horizons.

Today I passed innumerable pilgrims along the various trails doing the same thing. They were sitting as motionless as statues, legs crossed under them, hands in laps, staring out at apparently nothing at all. But here is a curious thing: on the faces of most of them was the same look of earth-detachment, curiosity, interest, delight, expectancy, peace, and contentment that I used to see on your face when you were looking out that way. I wanted to touch each one of them on the shoulder as I passed, and ask him if he would do me the favor of telling me just what he was seeing, or perhaps hearing, off there in those distances. But I didn't. Instead I walked reverently around them and continued on my way.

I can understand how those pilgrims might find happiness and satisfaction in what they were doing, but why you went in for this sort of thing still puzzles me. Watching you out of the corners of my eyes upon different occasions, I discovered that most of the time you were staring off into "empty space." It was just as though part of you were on the earth and another part, invisible to human eyes, stretched out "beyond the beyond." During those moments I always got the impression that you were probably in touch with verities unseeable by ordinary sight; perhaps making contact with creation as it really is back of the seeming. And who, I should like to ask, without the ability to see life as a dog sees it, and to understand life as a dog understands it, is qualified to say otherwise?

It may have been that you were looking out into that "empty space" with something far more perceptive than those two round things in the front of your head called "eyeballs". Humans are able to do this. So why not dogs? Every intelligent human knows that his range of actual vision extends illimitably beyond his physical eyesight, even though he may not do much about it. We have various names for this "other sight" apparatus: "the mind's eye, the inner eye, intellectual discrimination, contemplation, mental regard, discernment, rational power, spiritual awareness," and so on. The best examples of fine living in the human species are always found among those who have become proficient in the use of this incalculable inner endowment.

That humans do not make greater use of this

"vaster vision" is attributed to many causes. According to the metaphysical experts, who usually move about high above the earth levels, this slowness, or backwardness, comes from our failure to grasp the fact that all life is mental. From center to circumference purely mental. That each of us is a mental being in a mental universe. And that every phase of materiality, whatever its size, shape, or description, is merely "such stuff as dreams are made on."

I wonder if we humans appear as peculiar to you dogs, at times, as we do to ourselves! Obviously not, or you would not be so devoted to us. You probably see us as we ought to be. But here is a significant thing that is worth thinking about: no matter how materially successful, important, powerful, or influential humans become, they are never really satisfied. They never find the ultimate peak in their endeavors. "Something" within them is always disturbing them, making them restless, making them discontented. They may own much, they may be able to dominate and control many; but even this does not still an ever-haunting longing to drop the whole business, to escape from people, things, and even their skin bodies, and be free. Boundlessly free.

If there is sufficient receptivity they usually discover that that indefinable, disturbing "something" is not only all about them, but is gently and irresistibly pulling them upward and outward towards a greater, more satisfying, and more permanent sense of life than the one they have been experiencing along the earth levels. If they are wise they do not resist, but set their thinking and actions to moving in rhythm with it as best they can. In other words, they turn from the material setup and its functioning, and through mental endeavor seek to find and know more about that "something." That is why all the pilgrims are on Mount Hiei today. Each is mentally and spiritually exploring outward from his own particular "Mount of Vision." The ecstasy on their faces plainly indicated that they were taking in much more than scenic impressions. I can understand their purpose in this. But I wish I knew just what you saw, and what all the rest of you dogs see, when you stare off so earnestly into "empty space."

While the priest and I talked this afternoon, I asked him if he thought it ever would be possible for human beings to solve their appalling problems, especially those having to do with international affairs, and learn to live together in true neighborliness. "Yes," he said thoughtfully, "they will be solved, but only as each one of us solves them in his own heart. There is no other way. The world is made up of individual expressions of life. Each of us is one of those expressions, and is contributing his part; contributing it not so much by what he says and does, but by what he is. The best way to solve world problems is for each of us to perfect himself. If each of us lived a good life, there would be no world problems. In your country, in my country, in all countries, we attend religious ceremonies, read scriptures, chant and sing hymns, and meditate; but unless these things help us to live divinely, they are useless.

"Living divinely in everyday life is difficult. It takes courage, but the satisfaction it brings is worth it. Most people are content to submerge their divine individualities and live mass lives. That is always dangerous. Crowds usually pull us down to lower levels of ourselves—intellectually, artistically, emotionally, and morally. Crowds contract us. Crowds dim our vision. Crowds prevent us from finding and being our true selves. That is why the wise man escapes from the crowd whenever he can and, if it is possible for him to do so, flees to the mountains, or the desert, or the sea; and there in solitude communes with Nature, the universal mother, and learns the lessons She has to teach all those ready for the experience."

Then he lapsed into silence and we both stared off into "empty space." From out of the forest back of us came the deep reverberations of one of the big bronze temple gongs. To me, having heard these sounds most of the day, it was just another gong being beaten. But to the priest it was filled with meaning. He came abruptly out of his meditations, jumped to his feet, said a hasty goodbye with a blessing on the end of it, lifted the skirts of his robe to give his legs plenty of room, and sprinted into the forest as though he were out to establish some kind of a new world's record.

*I'll be seein' you*

# VAGRANT

*To*

*Strongheart*
*Eternal Playground*
*Out Yonder*

Dear old Pal:

When in the future anyone speaks to me of Kyoto, I shall not think immediately of the famous and very lovely historical city itself, nor of the variety of fine art objects made there, nor of the distinguished humans I met, but of a dirty little tramp dog. I met him early this morning while wandering around the outskirts of the city on a sight-seeing tour. Coming to a bend in the road I was tramping along, I stopped to look at an unusually beautiful sweep of countryside. From the opposite direction came several coolies hauling a heavily laden, two-wheeled cart. They seemed to like the view, too, for they stopped a short distance from me and began watching it like eager children.

Some minutes later a policeman appeared. He was too small to be imposing-looking, but nevertheless he bristled with self-importance and authority. The coolies had evidently stopped in the wrong place, for as soon as the policeman got near enough, he began shouting orders at them.

The coolies did not move. Instead they watched him with the same gentle, non-resisting expression one sees in the faces of cows. The policeman was annoyed. Evidently he was accustomed to immediate obedience whenever he barked out an order. Then I saw the dog. He was standing a short distance behind the policeman, watching him with silent but ominous intent. Trouble was brewing in more ways than one. Architecturally, the dog was a complete bungle. Neither the head, body, legs, ears, nor tail belonged in the same ensemble. He looked like something that had been hastily and carelessly thrown together from all sorts of left-overs. He was grotesque, battle-scarred, and incredibly soiled; but the spirit of defiance in him was magnificent. He looked ready and willing to fight the world, or any part of it, on any terms.

The policeman started angrily towards the coolies. When he was half way across the road, the dog charged. The little fellow's tactics obviously came from long experience in street warfare. He kept circling around the officer, ducking, twisting, weaving, and lunging and snapping at his ankles incessantly. The policeman kicked at him viciously, but that four-legged target was too fast. The policeman picked up a stone and threw it. The dog leaped sideways and resumed the attack. Finally, in a rage that sizzled in its fury, the upholder of law and order took a running kick at his assailant, missed, threw himself off balance, and landed flat on his back in the dust of the road. Hollywood would have called it "a perfect comedy flop."

His mission accomplished, the dog galloped down the road, flinging barks to right and left.

The coolies, with guarded grins, hurried to get their cart rolling again before reprisals set in, while the policeman made a retreat that must have embarrassed him to his heels. There was no chance for him to save face in the situation. An hour later I saw the dog again. He was barking at the ankles of bicycle riders. Two of them fell off sideways trying to kick him, while a fourth, after taking a header over his handlebars, eased his feelings by flinging his bicycle at the little irritant.

Later, I came to a large park. As I approached the red torii entrance something whizzed past me close to the ground. It was that dog again. He seemed to be haunting me. A short distance down the road, a man in a uniform I could not identify was leaning against a tree puffing heavily. He had been chasing the dog. In his hand was a club, which he threw with disgust against a nearby fence. I bought some cakes from an old lady who was selling them and hurried into the park. I had to know that dog. It was a long search, but I found him. He was sitting back of an ancient pagoda. His eyes were glassy, his tongue hanging out, and he was breathing heavily. I walked as near as I diplomatically dared, sat down on the grass, told him who I was, where I was from, what I was doing in Japan, and asked him if he and I could join forces and share an adventure or two together.

He eyed me with cold suspicion. I tossed a cake over near him. He ducked as though it had been a brick, but did not run away. I talked a continuous good-will monologue to him, stuffed with compliments for him. Poor little fellow, I do not suppose anyone had ever sent a friendly thought in his direction before. As I talked, I tossed cakes in his direction until they extended like little stepping-stones from near his left paw to my right knee. The cake-tossing intrigued him. He was evidently wondering why one of them didn't bounce off his head or body and cause pain.

After what seemed like a long stretch of time he nosed the nearest cake, looked at me suspiciously, sniffed again, and swallowed it whole. He liked it. They were good cakes; I liked them myself. He tried another, and then another. He was desperately hungry. At last he was close enough to take a sniff at me. He did it cautiously, keeping his body and legs flexible for a fast getaway if necessary. I sat as still as I could and let him handle the situation. He sniffed completely around me, then stretched out guardedly and gave the back of my hand a dainty dab with his tongue. I slowly reached over and stroked the back of his head. The barriers between us were down.

After that we toured the park together piling adventure upon adventure. Then we had a big meal, big for him and big for me, too. Now we are spread out under some trees taking our ease. He is asleep at the moment. I do not know where he has gone in his dreams, but if I may judge by the strange noises he is making in his throat and the twitchings of his ill-formed little body, he has the entire Japanese police force, as well as all the dog catchers in the empire, in full retreat. Watching him, it suddenly occurred to me that every human I had seen him bark and snap at had been wearing some kind of a uniform. Then I remembered how much you disliked uniforms, and how much other dogs I have known have disliked them too. I never saw you actually bite anyone in a uniform, but you always got plenty tough when anyone came around you with one of them on.

Now just what is the significance of all this? Are dogs anti-uniform? It would appear so. But why? Do you dogs object to the uniforms as garments? Or to the uniformity back of the uniforms? Could it be that you dogs are linked together in some kind of confederacy to get humans not only out of uniforms, but out of their rapidly increasing uniformity and conformity? Is it possible that you dogs, with your great affection for us, have sensed the danger we humans are drifting into with our willing consent to the regimenting of our minds and bodies, and are trying in the best way you know to drive us out of these lock-stepping habits for our own good? I wonder!

We humans believe, at least theoretically, that the universe functions on a plan of interrelated diversity; that each of us has been given a distinct and unique individuality; and that this individuality should be respected, cherished, honored, and guarded at all cost. But somehow or other we appear to lack the ability to demonstrate it. Few of us have the backbone to stand up frankly, courageously, boldly, steadfastly, and really be ourselves. Like this little tramp dog by my side, for instance. He hasn't much of anything to look forward to; his life is filled with difficulties and uncertainties; dangers beset him on every side; he apparently eats infrequently; he has neither home nor friends; and the world of humans is mostly antagonistic. And yet, in spite of these things, he has the courage to be himself; to live life in his own way; and to make existence, rough and uncertain as it is, yield him happiness, amusement, and satisfaction.

I wish it were possible to take him around the rest of the world with me as a travelling companion and tutor. I could learn something useful from him every hour of the day. True, he is only a dirty little mongrel. Just another pickup for the dog catchers. And yet I do not know one human who wouldn't be a better citizen of the universe with some of his dauntless spirit . . . his courage . . . his vitality . . . his honesty . . . his sincerity . . . his resourcefulness . . . his enthusiasm . . . his independence . . . his originality . . . his self-reliance . . . his fearlessness . . . his daring . . . his hardihood . . . his self-confidence . . . and his inner exultation. All he needs is an understanding human, with whom he can share his inner opulence.

*I'll be seein' you*

# POETS

*To
Strongheart
Eternal Playground
Out Yonder*

Dear old Pal:

I am cruising down one of the loveliest bodies of water in the world—the Inland Sea of Japan. The Japanese call it "The Poets' Sea," because of its colorful, lyrical, rhythmical configuration and atmosphere. Most of this day I sat in the bow of the ship watching ever-changing and ever-fascinating land- and seascapes. It was an exalting experience. But there were two flies in my ointment; two flies in the form of human beings, who sat on either side of me and talked incessantly. In a sense I was trapped between them, as I had the best chair position on the ship and it was a question of either finding a less desirable place, or remaining there and having to listen to their chatter. I remained.

Both of them, I gathered from their conversation, were poets. Not particularly good poets, I would imagine from what they said, but nevertheless poets, and poets riding down a poetical sea. They were engaging in what we humans call "discussion." Now, for your information, a discussion is supposed to be a mental and vocal activity in which those participating examine, reason about, and share ideas for the good of all concerned. But they were holding a sort of intellectual pole-vaulting contest, in which each was trying to top the other. They started quietly enough, but before long they were in heated controversy over what was, and was not, good poetry, flinging verbiage back and forth across me as though I might have been an over-stuffed slip cover on the chair. There was nothing I could do about it, except to be patient and wait for them to run down, which eventually they did, like two old grandfather clocks.

For some miles there was soothing silence. Then the one at my right suddenly turned and said to me, "Perhaps you will tell us your idea of good poetry?"

I had been expecting that sooner or later they would make an attempt to pull me into their arena, and had been preparing for just such an emergency. For a moment or two I pretended to be in deep reflection. Then I said "My idea of good poetry is any dog doing anything." I couldn't have startled them more if I had suddenly stood on my head and wagged my feet at them. I don't think they knew whether I was a mental case, sane and trying to insult them, or attempting to start some new kind of mutiny on the high seas. It could have developed into a social and literary incident of major proportions. But it didn't. You saved the day, as you always do whenever I bring you into situations of this kind. Telling them about you was master strategy, as both of them had seen you in pictures; both were dog owners, and both spent much time companioning with their dogs. They could not agree about poets and poetry, but when it came to dogs they saw eye-to-eye.

Calling any dog doing anything "good poetry," however, was so unorthodox and complicated for them that I had to make an explanation. I told them in brief that about the only thing I had heard them agree to was that poetry was one of the noblest and most delightful of all the forms of expression known to mankind. They nodded in approval. "By expression," I said, "I suppose you mean the pressing-out of one's inner feelings in the correct poetic form. The 'ex-pression' of an 'im-pression,' so to speak." Again they nodded. "It has been my observation," I continued, "that when the average human decides to poetize, he goes about it in a traditional routine common to all poets. After his feelings and emotions have bubbled up sufficiently for him to have the urge to press them out, he provides himself with writing equipment, finds a place to blend with his moods, and begins a laborious process of hunting for words with just the right sound and shades of meaning to suit his purposes. Then he goes through an arduous travail of setting these words down on paper in the conventionally correct way. The results, good or bad, he calls poetry." Again they nodded, but rather hesitantly, as though suspicious that I was leading them into a trap.

I asked if either of them had ever noticed the

natural poetic equipment possessed by every dog. They hadn't. I asked them if they had ever given serious study to the range and quality of a dog's awareness . . . its intelligence . . . its understanding . . . its imagination . . . its emotional response . . . its inner and outer vitality, rhythm, harmony and cadence . . . its unspoken eloquence . . . or its talent for influencing the thoughts, sentiments, and purposes of human beings? Neither of them had. At that moment I knew what was wrong with them. They liked dogs. They had great affection for dogs. They had been associating with dogs for a long time. But they had never really seen a dog. And I told them so. They still believed that the material form of a dog was all there was to a dog.

"When it comes to real poetry," I said to them, "you will find just as great poets and just as fine poems among dogs as you will among the human species. As a matter of fact, I am not beyond believing that the dogs surpass us in this particular form of artistry. Their methods of 'expression' differ; that is all. When a dog feels the urge to press out and share with others the emotions he feels, he is not handicapped by having to cramp and squeeze them through narrow form channels, like the human. Instead he turns his feelings full-on, and lets them flood through every fibre of his being. He composes a poem by turning himself into a poem, from the tip of his nose to the tip of his tail. The human writes poetry. The dog lives poetry. And who among us, in a Cosmos in which so much of reality has yet to be discovered, is qualified to say whether the human or the dog method of self-expression is nearer the ultimate of reality !"

I did not even wait for them to answer ."Strongheart was one of the most colorful and irresistible poets, and poems, I have ever known," I said to them. "The world proclaimed him a superlative because of his ability to be and 'ex-press' his own individuality and uniqueness. The world failed to understand, however, that all that 'greatness,' all that attractive outwardness was simply the nobility and beauty of his character diffusing themselves. In his pictures he was always his unspoiled self all the way through, no matter what they asked him to do. He was an animated poem moving among less poetic humans.

"It was not the plots of his films which stirred people so deeply, but the dog himself. He emancipated millions of men, women and children from monotonous and unsatisfying behavior patterns. He knocked their emotional skylights open and let in fresh air and sunshine. He took away for the time being their friction and discontent . . . broadened their sympathies . . . straightened their backbones for them . . . squared their shoulders . . . made their blood circulate better . . . lightened their footsteps . . . stimulated their better instincts . . . stirred their imaginations . . . restored their child-hearts to them . . . made them glow with real fun, excitement and laughter . . . added to the richness of their lives . . . helped them think better of themselves, their fellow-men, and all created things. Is there a human poet anywhere who wouldn't be proud and grateful to have accomplished that?"

Neither of them answered. They were staring out over the bow of the ship. Everyone on the deck had suddenly stopped talking. I sank into silence myself. We were sailing through a pink and purple sea, straight into a crimson and gold sunset. Off to the right a round yellow moon was just arising back of some fantastic little islands. The divine Poet back of all things was speaking through all things, and we had all become parts of His poem.

*I'll be seein' you*

# EXPLORERS

*Shanghai*
*China*

*To*

*Strongheart*
*Eternal Playground*
*Out Yonder*

Dear old Pal:

Adventures have been following one another in swift succession since arriving in China. Not that this is unusual, for China is pre-eminently a land of adventure and adventurers. It is an extraordinary country. A country of baffling contradictions, but alluring on whatever mental, moral or physical plane one cares to experience it. China is the only nation that knows how to be tranquil and turbulent . . . mellow-wise and foolish . . . sane and irresponsible . . . amusing and pathetic, at one and the same time. I know now why China creeps into one's heart and remains there.

This afternoon I attended a reception in honor of a distinguished traveler who is leaving for the Gobi desert. Never before had I seen so many adventurers gathered together within four walls. There was every known variety of professional risk-takers, from explorers with world-wide reputations to down-but-not-out soldiers of fortune, ready to join anyone on any kind of venture, and no questions asked. It was a rare occasion. For some time I moved slowly about the various rooms, fanning my ears like an African elephant, and picking up tales of reckless daring and incidental titbits. In one of the corners of the main room I came upon an unusually interesting-looking man, sitting by himself and watching the crowd with what seemed to be detached amusement. I joined him and for some time we talked in the impersonal, noncommittal manner that strangers have a way of doing in the Orient.

Finally, in an effort to find out who he was and what he did, I asked him where the most interesting adventures could be found at the present time. My guess was that he would recommend some novel kind of hunting in one of the Malay jungles. For some seconds he looked at me quizzically, as though adding and subtracting me into a temporary total. Then he said, "My personal preference is for sitting in an old-fashioned rocking chair, and exploring the undiscovered regions inside my own mind."

I almost upset a plateful of sandwiches a slant-eyed boy was holding in front of me. I had expected the unusual, but not to that degree. He laughed. "Don't be alarmed," he said, "I'm quite normal. The fact is I happen to be one of those things called an explorer. As an explorer I have been to nearly all of the out-of-the-way places that men of my profession like to go. And I have explored them thoroughly. We have conquered practically all of the geographical frontiers. But not the mental frontiers. We know almost nothing about the oceans and continents lying still undiscovered in the regions of our own minds. That is the real challenge to the adventurer and the explorer. Geographical exploration is simple and comparatively easy, if you have sufficient financial backing. Mental exploration is much more difficult. It takes more initiative, more daring, and more courage, because most of the way one has to go it alone. But its return in satisfaction is greater."

The room being too noisy for quiet conversation, he and I made a strategic retreat to my rooms on the top floor, where there was a balcony affording broad views of the animated Bund and the ever-colorful Whang-poo river. On the way through the living-room he stopped with an exclamation of delight. He had seen your picture. He knew who you were, and he is still one of your ardent fans, even though you no longer appear in motion pictures. He said that you were one of the few actors of all time that could really stir up people's imagination; and that you provided adventures for millions who were too mentally and physically lazy to provide adventures for themselves.

After we had arranged ourselves comfortably on the balcony, I told him that while I could understand his interest in exploring his own mind, the chair part of it puzzled me. "Why the old rocker?" I asked.

"Merely an idea of my own," he answered with twinkling eyes. "To understand its significance, it is necessary to remember that everything is in a state of continuous motion. Or vibration, if you prefer the term. Instead of remembering this, however, and recognizing that we have to move with this Cosmic force whether we like it or not, most of us try to disregard it. We feel that we are independent and unrelated items in the universe, privileged to do what we please, as we please, when we please—regardless of everything except ourselves. That is what starts all our trouble and grief.

"I use my old rocker to counteract this. I use it to rock myself into physical and mental rhythm with the universe. It is unorthodox, but effective. The Orientals know how helpful rocking can be in efforts of this kind, only they rock on their heels, or from a cross-legged sitting position, I prefer my old chair, not only for its comfort, but because whoever made it was a first-rate artist, with a first-rate artist's sensitive feeling for proportion, balance, and movement."

I asked him if he would tell me how he took off on his expeditions into the hinterland of his own mind. He was most willing.

"First," he said, "I place my body in the chair. Then I thoroughly relax, letting go of everything. Next I slow my breathing. Then I begin rocking back and forth, easily and slowly, keeping my thinking moving outward as much as possible. Gradually the picture of myself as a human being, anchored to the earth by a material body, fades away, and I become just my thinking, capable of moving to any distance without restrictions of any kind. Some people might call this meditation, but I prefer to call it mental exploring, for that is what it is. It is a hunt for new countries, or states of consciousness, in the great spiritual-mental universe lying undiscovered all about us, or more correctly, in us."

We paused to order dinner. Then he went on. "Although you might not think so by a casual look around the earth," he said, "it is nevertheless true that the world is more interested in mental exploration at the present time than at any other in its history. And for a very startling reason. The spiritual and material scientists are causing the material universe to disappear actually before our very eyes. These fellows are insisting, with ever-increasing proof, that the universe of mechanized matter, which each of us seems to see and experience external to himself, is not external at all, but inside of us; that is, inside each individual mind. And, what is even more disturbing, made of the same substance as mental ideas. They are proclaiming that everything contrary to a spiritual–mental universe is as temporary and fleeting as vapor."

I asked him why he thought it was that people were so reluctant to go adventuring in their own minds.

"There are probably all sorts of reasons," he answered, "but among them would be dread of the unknown . . . fear of change . . . lack of respect for one's individuality . . . no initiative . . . indifference . . . spiritual sluggishness . . . ignorance . . . prejudices . . . willingness to have others think and plan for them . . . and particularly, lack of imagination. Imagination is one of the most valuable faculties we have. But we neglect it shamefully. With imagination one can reach and experience the Infinite, but without it he becomes like a dead thing floating around and obstructing navigation. Children, before they are taught to be 'practical,' use this gift naturally and become delightfully self-contained. They ride out fearlessly on the wings of their imaginations to the most delectable and invigorating of worlds. We used to call these worlds of theirs fanciful, fabulous, and at times rather silly; but now the scientists are beginning to say that those worlds were probably nearer the ultimate reality than all the things that are happening, or have happened, on the speck in space we call the earth."

"Someone once wrote," I told him, "that the ways of imagination and vision are man's nearest approach to the ways of primordial Being."

"Another put it this way," he replied. "Blessed are the imaginative, for they shall go forward until they see God in everything, and all becomes Divine."

*I'll be seein' you*

# MISSIONARIES

*China Sea*

*To*
*Strongheart*
*Eternal Playground*
*Out Yonder*

Dear old Pal:

If I could turn my body into a cannon ball and have it shot, at the proper arc, out of the porthole through which I am looking, I would land on the pirate coast of China. With my power-glasses I can see just a dim outline of it through the darkness. It is a section of coast with mysterious indentations and inland waterways, out of which pirate ships slip stealthily at intervals to prey on coastwise shipping, plundering boats and carrying off people for ransom. They never molest foreign liners as large as the one I am on, but I noticed that the lower-class Chinese who came aboard at Shanghai were carefully searched for concealed weapons. A favorite ruse of the pirates, I am told, is to get aboard boats as passengers and capture them at sea.

I am on my way to Hong Kong with a shipload of diversified passengers, including a number of missionaries who have been attending a conference in Shanghai and are on their way back to their various stations in South China. As you probably never encountered one of them, let me tell you that a missionary, that is, a foreign missionary, is one who goes into countries other than his own to preach and teach his beliefs about God, man, and present and future life; and to improve, if possible, the mental, moral, physical, and social conditions of those who may need it. But, let me add, there are missionaries and missionaries, just as there are dogs and dogs.

My steamer chair is on the starboard deck amidships, and I am surrounded by missionaries. They are excellent company—gentle of manner and speech, considerate, unselfish, tremendously sincere in their efforts to be of service to their fellow-men, and as happy as a lot of boys on a picnic. Most of them live in remote places, where they seldom meet men who speak their language or have kindred ideas.

Tonight as I sat with them they talked shop, and I listened to heart-stirring, and even breath-taking, stories of heroism and sacrifice . . . of preachings and conversions . . . of spiritual and physical healings . . . of missionary work carried on in the face of almost overwhelming obstacles and hardships. There was no bragging, no self-exploitation, and no trying to top the other fellow's story, so customary in most human conversations. The things they talked about were dramatic, even sensationally so at times, but they were merely discussing their everyday jobs in an impersonal way.

Not once did I hear a negative remark. Not once was there a hint of complaint or criticism, or an admission of fear or discouragement.

Their talk was simple, but it was illumined by vision . . . purpose . . . friendship . . . and love; and motivated by the desire to share . . . help . . . heal . . . and bless. It was the kind of talk that the world would have been the better for hearing.

On towards midnight the missionary on my right startled me by asking if I would tell them about some of the missionaries I must have met in my travels. And was I on a spot! I did not have the remotest suspicion of being asked such a question and, to make it even more difficult, I could not recall ever having met a missionary before in my life. I mentally hopped all over my memory areas, but nary a missionary could I find. Then an idea popped, and I told them that, outside of themselves, the most interesting missionary I had ever known was a dog.

Every one of them went into a sudden mental tailspin. The situation became tense, quite frigidly so. Isn't it funny what giving a rational or fraternal rating to a dog will do to human beings at times? I did not mean to shock them. I had merely forgotten for the moment that others do not always see dogs as I do. "I meant no disrespect by bringing a dog into this," I said, noting the shocked look on their faces. "I have a very high regard for what a dog really stands for. Perhaps our definitions of missionaries differ. I was assuming, in a very elastic way of course, that a missionary is, at or least should be, a perfect exhibit of the God or gods he represents. And capable of influencing for the better everyone with whom he comes in contact, irrespective of their species . . . race . . . color . . . religious affiliation . . . politics

. . . philosophy . . . or social classification." Then with considerable detail I told them about you.

When I finished, the missionary who had asked the question said, with glowing good humor, "I am afraid you compel us to accept your dog pal as one of us. After all, a good missionary is simply a clear transparency for the glory of God to shine through; and that shining-through creates a spiritual environment, out of which each one he meets should be able to take what best suits his capacity and need. The need of the world today, probably more than at any other time in its history, is men who can live the good life so attractively that it inspires others to do likewise." I had another opening.

"That is why Strongheart was such a good missionary," I told them. "Like most dogs, he always lived life at his best levels. I never knew him to cheat or take holidays in this. True, he knew nothing about religion in the popular meaning of that term, nor did he have any set formulas about the correct way to live life; but his inner reservoirs overflowed with many of the things that true religion is supposed to symbolize. Wherever he went he preached the kinds of sermons that everyone could understand and profit by. He preached sermons in the most difficult way—by living them.

All the truth he knew, he put into action. He knew how to make the good life prevail, in spite of things. But what is more important, he had the ability to awaken some measure of good in everyone he met. And remember, he had no speech to help him. He had only his 'dumb' self.

That and his character and conduct. Living the best he was capable of without deviation, sharing the best he had without reservation, who shall say that that dog was not truly serving God . . . man . . . and the universe, that he was not truly doing good missionary work?"

For some time all of us sat silently looking off into the darkness. Then from a few chairs to the right, another one of the missionaries spoke.

"There is an old, old story about St. Francis of Assisi that fits in here," he said. "One day in his hillside monastery, the good saint asked a young monk to accompany him down into a nearby village and preach with him. Reaching the village, they walked the length of the main street and back again, and then returned to the monastery.

'But I thought we were going to preach,' exclaimed the young monk when they returned.

'We have been preaching,' St. Francis replied with a smile. 'We were preaching while we were walking. We have been seen . . . we have been looked at . . . and our behaviour has been noticed. We have delivered a morning sermon. It is no use to walk anywhere to preach, my son, unless we preach as we walk.' "

Which, my dear Strongheart, seemed to be a fitting climax for a perfect evening off the pirate coast of China.

*I'll be seein' you*

**126**

## CHINESE SEASONING

*Hong Kong*
*China*

*To*

*Strongheart*
*Eternal Playground*
*Out Yonder*

Dear old Pal:

The Chinese part of the 'round-the-world adventure is drawing to a close. I have seen, heard, touched, tasted, and sniffed all of China that I could. It has been an enriching experience. At the moment I am scribbling to you from the side of a hill which looks down upon Hong Kong and its famous harbor. Just astern of a British warship in the harbor is a broad-beamed Dutch steamer being loaded with cargo for the Dutch East Indies. When she heads seaward this afternoon I shall be aboard. It is winter here, but below the equator where we are going, it is summer. It is not the season one ordinarily selects for travel in the tropics, for aside from the heat, it is the typhoon season. But winter or summer, typhoons or no typhoons, when that Dutchman leaves, I leave too.

I wish I could remain in China for an indefinite time, as the country has been teaching me much that it is good for me to know, good for every Occidental to know. If I could remain, I would like to scuttle present plans and return to an ancient mandarin house not many miles from here, and let the old house give me additional lessons in the art of cultural living. It is one of the finest teachers I have met in China, even though classified by my species as an "inanimate thing." But even "inanimate things" have great truths to share with us, when we are ready for the experience, haven't they!

Getting to the house is an adventure in itself, as the route lies through streets and bazaars dense with humanity, around corner after corner, and over hill and dale. The first time I started there I was sure the guide had lost his way, even though he assured me that the "favorable omens of heaven" were with us. After considerable serpentine footwork we came to an ordinary-looking old door in a long stretch of old-looking high wall. The guide knocked. Nothing happened. After awhile he knocked again. Nothing happened. This went on for some time. He was not in the least discouraged or annoyed. But, then, time meant nothing in his life, and besides, he had been nurtured on the tradition that with patience and good humor one may conquer all things, even heaven.

Eventually the door squeaked inward, and there was the mandarin house in all its architectural splendor, nestling in a quiet, peaceful garden filled with color and heavy with perfume. Every part of that ancient house, its flowing lines and curves, its walls, its floors, its ceilings, its decorations, and its furnishings, proclaimed the exalted greatness of the artists and craftsmen who brought them into human visibility from out of the realm of their inspired imaginations. Those masters of mind, and of heart, and of hand, may have disappeared beyond the range of our material senses, but something very fine that was not only theirs, but they themselves, is still vividly and eloquently here, for our edification and encouragement. Having something worth saying, they said it, and the centuries applaud them.

Each room has a special motif, with appropriate mottoes, proverbs, or quotations from the classics painted on the walls. My favorite room looked out into a quaint little boxed-in courtyard with a lily fountain in the center, where the only sounds were the trickling water, the birds, bees, and singing crickets. The room was known as "THE ABODE OF TRANQUILITY." Over one door was the motto, "WHEN THE HEART IS BALANCED THEN THERE IS JOY," and over the courtyard door this: "WHY GO OUT OF DOORS WHEN THE WHOLE WORLD IS WITHIN?" The adjoining room is "THE ABODE OF CONTENTMENT." Its wall mottoes are "LET THE DESIRES BE FEW AND THE HEART WILL FLOURISH," and "CLOUDS PASS AWAY BUT THE BLUE HEAVEN LINGERS ON."

I have come to the conclusion that it is the spirit behind the form and the action which gives to China its enduring vitality and charm. I wish I knew how to capture and extract the pure essence of it for export purposes. To be able to put it into capsule form, for instance, for the benefit of Occidentals. What a blessing it would be for Western civilization if it were possible for the average citizen to swallow a capsule and immediately acquire real Chinese culture . . . wisdom . . . humor . . . intuition . . . artistic insight . . . common sense . . . patience . . . tranquility . . . courtesy . . . tolerance . . . contentment . . . appreciation . . . frankness . . . simplicity . . . good will . . . skill in conserving spiritual and physical energies . . . capacity for the enjoyment of commonplace things . . . and the ability to smile and go on, whatever happens, or doesn't happen!

But there is another way that would be more attractive and practical. I could export these fine qualities in chows and Pekingese. Those valiant little dogs carry the spirit of ancient China about as well as anything I know. Everything is in their favor. They come of ancient, illustrious lineage . . . they have been an intimate part of the nation's history . . . they possess high moral excellence . . . they move with a dignity befitting their traditions . . . they are natural philosophers . . . they respect their own independence and point of view . . . they are friendly, but discriminating . . . and they have many other qualities of the highest excellence. Yes, they would do. They could teach the rest of the world why it is that China has always been such a great nation; that is, they could if the humans were receptive enough.

I hadn't realized before I came here what splendid Chinese ambassadors these chows and Pekingese really are. Ambassadors not only of good will, but instructors in the almost forgotten science and art of living with nobility, graciousness, charm, and dignity. Now, among the human species, an ambassador is supposed to be one who represents and speaks for his country in a foreign land; one who helps maintain cordial relationships between the peoples of the two countries. Naturally, there are all kinds of ambassadors. I have known many of them, but I have never met one yet that I didn't feel would have been a better representative of his species, as well as his country, with some real dog qualities mixed in with his own, and the courage to keep them in outward circulation.

And speaking of these things, let me add that you were probably the most interesting ambassador that Germany ever sent to the United States. The others, the two-leggers, may have surpassed you in such things as political deals and social activities, but not in genuine interest, or in creating and maintaining good will. You may have had the advantage of motion pictures, but I doubt if any of them could have surpassed you in winning people's admiration and affection, even if the ambassadors had appeared in movies themselves. You see, Strongheart, you stood for the things that people of all countries admire and respect, even though they may live them indifferently in their own lives. You spoke a language that people of all nations could understand. It came from your heart, it went to hearts, and it came back from hearts. You would have been a complete failure as a political ambassador, however, even if you had been able to speak human language. You were too genuine, too sincere, too loyal to life itself. You lacked the ability to pretend. You had no talent for guile and duplicity.

I believe it would be helpful and constructive for "our civilization" if men who go in for public office and who direct the activities of others were required to spend more time with the dogs of their respective countries. I don't mean spending time with them as pets, but strictly in the interest of broadening and deepening the education of the human. Considering all the wise and important things you dogs have to share with us, isn't it shocking how little we humans have learned from you! This lapse probably comes from a quite general human inability to see a dog as anything more than a dumb, material thing, with a head, body, tail, and four legs, and something on the inside animating it.

Now I have to stop scribbling. In the road below is a laughing Chinese boy waving his arms to tell me that it is time for me to go. With him are several laughing assistants. This certainly is the "laughingest" country I have ever been in. The boys have two rickshas, one for my body and the other for my baggage. They are a picturesque-looking outfit. As soon as the final dot gets on this letter I shall join them, and they will transport me through the crowded streets of Hong Kong and see that I am deposited in the shore boat of that stout-ribbed Dutch steamer out there in the harbor.

*I'll be seein' you*

132

# "CHINKS"

South China Sea

To

Strongheart
Eternal Playground
Out Yonder

Dear old Pal:

Just how many days I have been cruising down the South China Sea aboard this broad-of-beam Dutch steamer is too weighty a problem to be worked out at the moment. Time has practically disappeared—as it should—except for those who have to attend to the navigating and the needs of the engines; and life is just one smooth, uninterrupted continuity of serene, lazy loafing. For the first few days the tail of a typhoon lashed the ocean into a furious mood, and we were knocked everywhich way except upside down. But all that is past now and we are sailing through glass-like water, with gorgeous color phantasies decorating sky and sea throughout each twenty-four hours.

We have a capacity cargo aboard. In addition, we are carrying an assortment of one thousand Chinese coolies to various islands of the Dutch East Indies. They are booked to labor in mines and on plantations and land developments. There are only three of us on the first-class passenger list. There would have been more but this is the typhoon season and people are not particularly fond of riding these seas at this time of the year. Even experiencing the flick of the tail of one of them was a nautical eye-opener for me. As there are so few of us on the first-class list, I have an entire row of cabins at my disposal, and the starboard side of the deck all to myself. It is like being on a private yacht.

Life aboard ship is the full flowering of the art of agreeable dawdling. There is nothing to do and there is expert assistance in doing it. At six o'clock in the morning a smiling Chinese boy awakens me by gently stroking a soft-toned gong. Another brings me black, pasty, Java coffee. Another toast. Another prepares my bath. Another lays out my clothes for the day—a pair of shorts and an undershirt. Another, the No. 1 boy, stands by supervising it all and entertaining me with amusing small talk about this and that.

At eight I am ceremoniously escorted into the dining-room, where I share "big breakfast" with the officers. Then I stroll slowly to my favorite deck chair, where I do nothing all morning but think in two-four time and watch sea-gulls, whales, flying fish, sharks, color effects, and the coolies on the deck just below mine. At eleven I am fed hot chocolate by a miniature army of attendants. At one o'clock there is "big luncheon." From two until four a siesta period is religiously observed by everyone except the working crew. At five I am fed tea, sandwiches, and cake. At seven-thirty there is "big dinner," and by nine practically everyone is sound asleep.

From where my steamer chair is placed I can

134

watch the coolies day and night, even though their deck has a canvas covering to keep off the hot rays of the sun. The coolies are packed almost solid from rail to rail, and there they cook, eat, sleep, visit, and play their games. I never knew before that human beings could exist in such close formation. The coolies are listed as "cheap, unskilled labor," and are valued chiefly for their willingness and ability to work long hours at hard, disagreeable tasks without complaint and for very little money. "Chinks!" they are called. "Just so many Chinks!" Employers order them by lot— like cattle.

Watching them one afternoon, it suddenly occurred to me that those coolies were actually getting more genuine satisfaction out of life than any collection of people I had ever seen anywhere. The more I watched them the more intriguing this became. Why, I wondered, were those coolies so happy, with so little to make them so? Were they unusually wise? Or unusually stupid? I stopped one of the ship's officers and put the question up to him. He focussed a pair of wind-blown blue eyes on me rather vaguely, paused, and in the best English he could muster, said "Why . . . er . . . er . . . yes, sir! That is correct, sir! Thank you, sir!" And off he marched, obviously pleased over being of service to a patron of the line.

Then I got permission to visit the coolies. There were exactly ten companionway steps between my deck and theirs, but the mental and emotional distance between them was enormous. Those ten steps took me completely out of the Occident and into the very heart of the Orient. I was not only in an entirely different world, but an entirely different state of existence. Behind me was a world of desire, all around me a world of contentment. Back of me was a world of overgeared, overtense efficiency; of confusion and disorder; of frustration and discontent; of political and economic frenzy; of war and threat of war. A world of bad manners. A world struggling desperately to function on the philosophy of the survival of the strongest and the slickest. A world burning up its energies with speed, greed, excitement, excesses, and follies. A world scrambling for personal rewards. A world drunk with power, fame, and wealth. A world saturated with unhappiness and misery.

But there were none of those things among the coolies. Life with them moved in an opposite direction. They were only "cheap man power," ordered like cattle, herded like cattle, shipped like cattle, and treated like cattle. Their worldly goods were few and light enough to be carried by hand. They had no comforts. They were even stripped of many of the things Occidentals call "ordinary necessities for living." But every one of them seemed to possess peace of mind, happiness, and satisfying experience in abundant degree.

Moving about their deck took deft navigation, as most of the space was covered with heads, torsos, legs, arms, and hands. But with patience and good footwork I managed it. No one seemed over-curious about me. If they looked at me at all, they smiled good-naturedly, made room for me, and went on with what they were doing. Everywhere was neighbourliness of an exceptionally high quality. Happiness . . . sincerity . . . frankness . . . gentleness . . . friendliness . . . sympathy . . . unselfishness . . . good humor . . . and laughter flowed from them as naturally and refreshingly as song from a bird, or perfume from a flower.

Gradually I came to see that existence with "those Chinks" meant wholehearted coöperation with the group. But coöperation in which apparently there was no interference with individual expression. They were a graphic illustration of collective individualism actually working. And without squeaking. They did not need external things to make them happy; for, like dogs, and children, and poets, and artists, and philosophers, and sages, and saints, they carried their happiness on the inside. Their wealth was not affected by the fluctuations of political or economic thermometers.

It was interesting to watch them adjust themselves to the experience of the moment. It seemed so easy for them. But, then, their world was childlike and basically good; it was a world filled with appreciation for common things and common pleasures; a world in which there was no recognition of hardships and difficulties; a world in which no one regarded life as a problem. Mentally, and almost entirely so physically, they lived naked and unashamed; so, having nothing to conceal, there was nothing for them to defend or row about, and no need for anyone to pretend.

As I visited their various decks—with senses

wide open—I did not see an antisocial or an unhappy expression on a single face. Nor did I find a trace of self-reproach . . . regret . . . discouragement . . . suspicion . . . unkindness . . . disappointment . . . bitterness . . . or ill will. They were doing what you dogs do—accepting life full-on, just as it came along, and making it yield them entertainment and happiness, in spite of things. And they were doing it together, let me add. No wonder they were at peace! No wonder they were having such a good time! No wonder they could laugh so heartily with or at the world!

Someone once said that whenever a man strikes a note of truth, whether he does it knowingly or unknowingly, he produces harmony for himself, his fellows, and his environment because he sets in vibration a universal chord. Isn't that illuminating! I shall never think of that statement again without being reminded, with a glow of gratitude in my heart, of a thousand half-naked Chinese coolies, packed like cattle aboard a Dutch steamer in the South China Sea, who taught me how that great universal chord may be kept in vibration.

*I'll be seein' you*

# YARDSTICKS

Batavia
Java

To
Strongheart
Eternal Playground
Out Yonder

Dear old Pal:

Having explored Java in almost every way that one can explore the island, I beg leave to report that the most astonishing thing seen to date is a human being from my own country. At the moment he is strutting about the hotel grounds where men and women, mostly Dutch, are sitting at little tables sipping cool drinks with formal precision, and listening to the music of a Russian orchestra. When I tell you that he is just completing the prodigious feat of revaluing and retagging all the animals in creation, you may get some idea of his rarity. He is about to announce formally to the world where all animals rightly belong in the scale of intelligence.

Professionally speaking he is a professor of animal physiology and psychology, a big-game hunter, and a taxidermist. Translated that means he is supposed to have expert knowledge about the outsides and insides of animals; to understand what makes them function and why; and to be able to kill and stuff them for exhibition and study purposes. For the past year he has been in Eastern jungles at the head of a subscription expedition killing animals, examining their organs, and measuring their brains to discover "their degree of intelligence." Last year he took the domestic animals apart.

Several of us visitors to Batavia had dinner together tonight, and the professor was one of us. I wondered who he was when I saw him earlier in the day, as he was dressed like a movie explorer, and acted as though an invisible sound camera were following him about and recording everything he did and said. He was quite the vainest thing I have seen outside of Hollywood. One look at him would have assured almost anyone that the professor had never been encouraged when young to play and have fun, and was without much of a sense of humor.

The dinner conversation had not proceeded far before the professor ran away with it and turned it into an informal lecture about himself and his explorations. In the beginning it was rather enlivening entertainment, as he was a good showman and a fluent talker; but as I began listening more to his thinking processes than to the pleasant word sounds he was making, I discovered that while he was talking with much eloquence, he was saying almost nothing at all, at least, nothing worthwhile. He was using a gorilla trick—beating his chest and making sounds come out through a hole in his head.

He wasn't really interested in animals, but in himself. He was using animals to build up a reputation for himself. To make a good living. He did not understand animals except in a superficial way. He couldn't. He had no genuine love for them. And most intelligent people know how impossible it is to understand anything in creation unless one loves it. To the professor, creation was a material arrangement of struggling biological groups, graded up and down an evolutionary scale, with the human species at the top dominating all the others. He regarded animals as relatively unimportant forms of flesh to be used in whatever manner suited his purposes. He had killed, dissected, and stuffed innumerable domestic and wild animals, but in all that destruction and research he had never been able to find even a trace of—well, let us call it—"that something" which gives to each living entity its life, being, intelligence, and capacities, and links us all together in the great totality of existence.

He told us, with much pride, how he had rearranged the scale of animal intelligence and given most of the animals new ratings. I thought you dogs would be up around the top somewhere, but you weren't. He had you pegged below elephants, beavers, horses, sea-lions, cats, and a number of other things. I asked him why he didn't give you dogs a better listing. "They don't deserve it," he said with finality and a wave of his hand.

"Why not?" I asked. The question annoyed him. He was evidently accustomed to talking without being interrupted or having his verdicts questioned.

"Most people," he said, and he looked as if he meant me in particular, "are sentimental about dogs, and their sentiments cause them to overrate dogs. In a limited degree the dog has emotional response, sensations, motor impulses, and can be trained to do certain not particularly important things, but its intelligence is definitely restricted. They belong just where I've put them!"

He waved his hand in an outward arc as though dismissing that particular point and me, too. It was a perfect moment in which to bring you in and, if you will pardon the slang, smack him down by challenging him to lay that silly little yardstick of his on you, and then try to explain how, with your "limited intelligence," you had been able to develop such remarkable capacity for independent thinking . . . reasoning . . . arriving at conclusions . . . reflection . . . and exchanging rational ideas with human beings. He couldn't have dismissed you with a wave of his hand. Or treated you casually. Your success was too conspicuous. You were too widely known for your accomplishments. But I didn't smack him down. It wasn't worth the effort. My mental antennas told me that.

I wish it were possible to reverse the procedure so that a commission of dogs could examine the professor, and rule on his intelligence and general worth from their point of view. Wouldn't that be amusing! And revealing! You could be the chairman, as your discriminating perception would be valuable in that position. Then, to make the commission international and broad in its judgments, you might have on the board with you an English bulldog, a German dachshund, an Italian greyhound, a Rusian wolfhound, a

Brussels griffon, a Spanish pointer, a Labrador retriever, a Norwegian elkhound, a Swiss St. Bernard, an Arabian saluki, an Arctic samoyed, an Irish setter, and a Portuguese sheep dog.

It wouldn't be necessary for the dogs to kill him, and examine his organs and brain to arrive at a fairly accurate estimate of him. A look, a sniff, and a momentary mental "feel" by you or any of those dogs suggested for your commission, and the professor would be "correctly listed," wouldn't he? It wouldn't be necessary to have him stuffed for exhibition and study purposes, either. He doesn't warrant it architecturally. Nor would it be fair to judge him by dog standards, especially those having to do with physique, physical ability, and moral outlook.

The equitable thing would be for the dogs to judge him entirely by human standards of what he considers himself to be—an educated gentleman. For the educational part of that term, he has documents to show that he attended a variety of public and private schools and was graduated from a college. The dogs would have to determine to what degree he is really educated. Presumably he was sent to all those schools to be educated all over. But was he? That is what you dogs would have to decide. He probably has intellectual proficiency, but what about his spiritual . . . esthetic . . . emotional . . . moral . . . and social development! Ah, there would be some fine points for you dogs to pass on.

As for the "gentleman" part of the educated gentleman, let me simply say that a gentleman is the male of the human species in his finest and fullest flowering. A gentleman, it is generally agreed, is one who not only has qualities valuable to society, but upholds them . . . who keeps the best of himself constantly flowing outward . . . respects all life . . . never inflicts pain, directly or indirectly . . . and who wishes for others the same good he enjoys for himself. Great men are always gentlemen and, like you dogs, great sharers. They usually live at their circumference, instead of around a personal center. They always have courage to be themselves. And they invariably leave the world better, happier, kindlier, and holier for their presence in it.

How is that for a measuring yardstick! I wonder how the professor would rate after being measured by it! But then, I wonder how I would rate myself!

*I'll be seein' you*

# PARADISE

*Don Pasar*
*Bali*

*To*

*Strongheart*
*Eternal Playground*
*Out Yonder*

Dear old Pal:

With your fur coat clipped off you would be a strange-looking object, but that is the only way you could enjoy Bali, because of the heat. Remember, Bali is below the equator and I am down here in the summertime. I wear almost nothing at all and even that is too much in the daytime. You would like Bali. Everybody and everything likes Bali. It is one of the few spots left on earth where the child-heart still blossoms in profusion. It is like something out of a highly imaginative story book. A fabulous place where no one ever really grows up. A land of abiding sunshine, beauty, fragrance, abundance, peace and joy. A tourist's mecca where Occidental perspectives are turned upside down and inside out.

Geographically, Bali is an overnight sail from the island of Java. Actually, though, it is a "Never, Never Country." One steps ashore, looks about him, gasps, and automatically exclaims, "It just can't be true!" My guide books list the island's three leading attractions as the native women, the native entertainment, and the scenery—in that order. The women are considered the most beautiful dark-skinned beauties in the world. They seldom wear clothes above their waistlines, and move with a rhythm and grace often seen in animals, but seldom in humans. Much of this comes, I am told, from carrying heavy loads on their heads. One of these animated poems is passing now. She has a large tray balanced on her head, like a fantastic spring hat, piled high with garden produce and cocoanuts. She seems to be gliding along the surface of the earth. She is chewing betel nut and tobacco.

The native entertainment goes on day and night. Very little of it is arranged for visitors. It is by natives, for natives, and is free. It includes concerts by their justly famous gamelang orchestras, which consist of percussion instruments, gongs, and bells played by men and boys guided entirely by intuition and inspiration; shadow-plays with cardboard actors, a light, and a sheet—the forerunner of the modern movies; mask dramas, puppet shows, theatrical performances in which whole villages take part; and varieties of dramatic, social and religious ceremonies.

One of the most interesting things about the Balinese is that they have been able to resist all efforts to educate them away from their individual and collective childhearts. While the rest of the world has been "growing up" in worldly sophistication, and perfecting itself in the tricks of competitive, acquisitive living, these gentle people have remained simple, natural, and light-hearted, sharing and enjoying together the beauty and the bounty of their part of the earth. Which probably explains why they still have a paradise in a strife-filled world.

It is said that there are no bad people on the island. That is understandable. There is no reason for anyone being bad here in such pleasant surroundings, and among such neighborly people. They seem to know that there is enough of everything for everyone, as long as they flow along together as a totality of mutual interests. And this they do, each contributing his particular talent to the common good and the common happiness, like happy, care-free children. They have never been snared into the quite general fallacy that the world is an arena in which everyone has to struggle with everyone else. They treat the earth like a glorified picnic ground. Every day is a holiday with them.

Perhaps this is why almost every Balinese is a sculptor, a painter, a musician, a poet, a dancer, an actor, or an artist in some other form of expression. Each contributes his individual part to the communal work, and then interests himself in whatever art expression he likes best. They do not create or perform for commercial purposes, but rather to let an irrepressible and irresistible Withinness express itself. All their art is public property. Talent flows from them as spontaneously and naturally as perfume from a flower, song from a bird, laughter from a child, and affection from a dog.

Not so long ago as humans record time, the Occidental world regarded the Balinese as "poor

147

benighted heathens." That is, they were considered to be in a more or less hopeless state of spiritual, moral, and intellectual darkness. Having decided this, the Occident, with its inordinate zeal for reforming and regulating others, began sending missionaries here to do something about the situation. The results, I am told, were effortful but not as productive as hoped for. It may have been that the Balinese were living the Christian virtues, especially those having to do with brotherly love and neighborly generosity, so much better than the missionaries had anticipated that there wasn't much for them to go to work on.

The Balinese do not need a costly government to compel them to be thoughtful and considerate. They like to be thoughtful and considerate. They like to share themselves, and what they have, with others. The world about them may rage with selfishness, greed, animosity, and conflict, but the Balinese live on under the impression that man is a social being, in a social community, a social world, and a social universe. Perhaps in their primitive, unclouded way they comprehend better than the rest of us that, back of the seeming, all reality of necessity is social.

Wouldn't it be an interesting twist in the scheme of things if the self-satisfied but befuddled Occident, not knowing where it is going or why, was compelled to come to these "poor benighted heathens" to learn how to be neighborly, productive, and happy at one and the same time! The Ballinese know how to do this, and they do it as naturally and as easily as children at play.

World teachers have been warning humans in season and out to cherish their child-hearts if they want to experience true happiness and blessedness. By child-heart they mean all those lovely qualities that only a child's soul symbolizes. Such, for instance, as simplicity . . . candor . . . purity . . . faith . . . naturalness . . . gentleness . . . present-mindedness . . . appreciation . . . enthusiasm . . . courtesy . . . honesty . . . sweetness . . . the ability to act without calculation . . . joy . . . confidence in good . . . unselfishness . . . the will to share . . . friendliness . . . sympathy . . . affection . . . teachableness . . . spontaneity . . . receptivity . . . inner flexibility . . . and the priceless ability to live abundantly, without possessing anything at all.

Those far-visioned teachers insist that in the degree the human loses these qualities, in just that degree does he lose his hold on reality, his ability to be and express his real selfhood, his aptitude for living, his value as a citizen of the universe, and his sense of the divine Togetherness forever existing between Creator . . . Created . . . and Creation. Then, they insist, he is automatically plunged into the darkness and chaos of humanity's most pernicious error—the illusion of disunity. They believe that there is only one way out of this dilemma. That is for each human to regain his pristine child-heart, and with gladness, fun, and laughter do his full part toward restoring the world to its original purity, simplicity, and goodness.

*I'll be seein' you*

# JUNGLES

*To*

*Strongheart*
*Eternal Playground*
*Out Yonder*

Dear old Pal:

I am now in Singapore—the "crossroads of the world." Singapore, where East goes West and West goes East, and everyone is at least discreet, if not always wise. At the front door is the sea, at the back door the jungle, and in the city, a colorful and ever-fascinating blending of Occident and Orient at their best and worst. Adventure beckons from all directions, especially to those with a fancy for stepping out of their customary, conventional ways of thinking about life and living it.

Let me share with you one I had yesterday. I had been exploring a nearby jungle and had stopped in a clearing to rest my feet. It was an unusual place, bordered by dense vegetation up through which grew large trees, their branches intertwining overhead and forming a green ceiling through which the sunlight just managed to penetrate with weird color effects. It was just the kind of place that hobgoblins would have chosen for their initiations and revels. The silence was intense, except when an occasional animal called out or hurried by.

In the midst of my peaceful reflections a great hullabaloo broke out all around me. The trees were alive with chattering monkeys. This went on for some time. Then an oldish-looking monkey came out from behind a tree, waddled cautiously to the center of the clearing, sat down, and began looking at me intently. I kept perfectly still and tried to make-believe I was part of the tree against which I was leaning. Another monkey dropped into the clearing and sat down. Then another and another, until the ground was covered with them. I would have given almost anything to have understood what they were talking about.

Suddenly, as though by a prearranged signal and without the least tip-off, every monkey went into action. Each seemed to break loose his imagination and comicality, turn his energy full-on, and let himself go without regard for results. The trees, the clearing, the very air itself became filled with highly animated little bodies moving swiftly in all directions. It was truly a super-marvelous performance. I have seen many gymnastic and athletic performances in different parts of the world, but never before have I witnessed such perfect coördination and control of skin-and-bone bodies. Their agility, dexterity, timing, precision, grace, and skill in motion were flawless. And it was just as funny as it was spectacular.

It bothered me, though, wondering how it was that I, supposed to be such a superior creature to a monkey, was so inferior to them in almost everything they were doing. My pride as a member of the human species was hurt. Those monkeys were altogether too good. So much so that if they had invited me to join them in their fun, I couldn't have done so. Why, I doubt if I could have chinned myself half a dozen times, to say nothing of leaping from tree to tree, and racing up and down them, the way they were doing. I was only an awkward, clumsy earth-footer, and not as superior as I had been believing.

In the midst of the show there was a series of sharp explosions a short distance away. Instantly every monkey vanished. More explosions. This time they were nearer. Then into the clearing bumped an ancient but still honorable automobile. It came from the direction of Singapore and was following the jungle road which cut through the clearing. At the wheel was a man wearing a cork helmet, khaki shorts, and boots. Two short-haired dogs of mixed lineage sat beside him. The back part of the car was filled with camp gear and supplies.

He stopped when he got near where I was, shouted a breezy "hello" and got out to let his engine cool. I could never have guessed what he was doing in the jungle with that outfit. He had none of the characteristics of a government official. He didn't look like a big-game hunter. And his eyes were too honest and humorous for a fugitive. As we talked I began getting snatches of his biography. He had been an exploring engineer. He had retired. He made his home on the shores of a lake some distance in the jungle. He was on his way home.

I asked him why he chose to live in a jungle. "They are pleasanter and safer," he answered.

"Safer?" says I.

"Yes, safer," says he. "If a man minds his own business, and behaves himself as he should, he is much better off with wild animals and natives for neighbours than he is living in civilized places with all those predatory human animals prowling around him. I never even carry a gun in the jungle. It isn't necessary. The only time I go armed is when I leave the jungle and live among my own species.

"People have wrong notions about the jungle. Jungles aren't geographical. They are states of mind and heart. We carry jungles around with us, inside of us. That is why so many jungle natives and animals are so much farther out of the jungle than millions of people who call themselves civilized. But don't take my word for it. Look around for yourself, and you will see that while civilization has been spreading rapidly in geographical jungles, jungles are spreading much more rapidly in geographical civilization. You can figure it out in whatever way you like, but if you do it thoroughly enough, you will come to understand why I prefer the jungle and peace of mind.

"Jungle life is often cruel, to be sure, but not as cruel as civilized life. The undisciplined human being is the most lawless and destructive thing on earth, particularly when he runs with a national, racial, political, religious, or economic pack. He can be more viciously depraved than anything the jungle contains. Why, those jungle natives and wild animals wouldn't tolerate much of the stuff that goes on in our modern cities. As a matter of fact, those natives and animals have some of the finest social and moral codes in existence. But few jungle travelers look for them."

I was interested in knowing his real reason for not carrying a gun with him in the jungle. What he told me in considerable detail, I will set down here briefly. Said he, "Years ago an old chief and I became close friends. One day he told me, using a few English words and much pantomime, that whatever went out from my heart would boomerang back at me from everything in the jungle. At first I did not grasp just what he meant. Then I discovered that natives and animals were reacting to my mental and physical attitudes towards them in the most astonishing way. The old chief was right. Whatever I sent out was coming back at me—like for like.

"After much experimenting, I learned at firsthand how sensitive most natives and animals are to mental impressions, or thought vibrations going through the air, or hunches, or whatever you please to call them. I discovered that the animals usually knew I was moving in their direction long before they could hear or see me, or even pick up my scent. They always seemed to know, too, whether I was coming as friend or enemy, and acted accordingly.

"There is nothing in the least mysterious about it. It is simple, elemental. The natives and animals have not been spoiled by certain bad features in our kind of education. For instance, they do not know that news and information of

154

importance to them are supposed to travel only through certain material mediums. Not knowing this, they listen to themselves, as you and I listen to a radio. Or as some people listen to and follow hunches. That is why natives always know so much about travelers coming their way long before arrival. It is a natural and important function that most civilized people have let go to waste.

If I go into the jungle armed, I am a potential killer, and I mentally broadcast that news to animals near, far, and wide. They may not always pick it up, but usually they do. If I am unarmed, there is no mental threat of danger or death broadcasting itself from me, and the animals assume an entirely different attitude towards me. It is what the old chief meant by the 'boomerang back.' That is why I never go armed. And that is why I seldom experience any difficulties with natives or animals. A good neighbor finds good neighbors wherever he goes, even in the jungle."

Then we said goodbye. He climbed into his car, gave it the gas and, after more noise than any mechanical thing ought to make, headed down the bumpy, snake-like road in the general directon of his jungle home by the lake. I set my feet moving towards Singapore, seriously pondering which of us was really heading for civilization.

*I'll be seein' you*

## "BEHOLD THE BIRDS"

*Bay of Bengal*

*To*
*Strongheart*
*Eternal Playground*
*Out Yonder*

Dear old Pal:

The Bay of Bengal, which I am cruising across now on my way to Ceylon, is one of the most temperamental bodies of water in the world. When the weather is fine, one sails through glass-like seas of enchanting loveliness with rainbow effects in all directions; but when it isn't, and the climatic moods change with almost unpredictable suddenness, one is apt to experience weather "as is weather." A few days ago the ship nosed into one of these turbulent moods and gave the passengers a ride they are going to remember for some time to come. The wind came in violent gusts, kicking up a heavy sea and blowing rain against the ship almost horizontally. The thunder and lightning were sensational.

I watched from a sheltered place on the top deck where I had an unobstructed view of sky, sea, and the plunging, rolling course of the ship. During one of the squalls two bright-colored objects came blowing along the deck, bumped against part of the deck house and stopped. At first I thought they were balls of yarn that had been blown out of some passengers' work-basket, but as I walked over to pick them up I discovered they were two little jungle birds. Their plight was apparent. They had been blown off shore by the recent gales, and our ship was probably the first solid object to land on they had been able to find in 'many, many hours of forced flying. They lay motionless on their backs with their tiny, delicate legs skyward. They were out cold.

A friend and I gave them first aid, provided them with a good nurse, and by morning they were flying merrily around one of the cabins, filling it with their anthems of gratitude and praise. Towards noon, when the weather was pleasant once again, the wind favorable, and land not too far away for flight, we took them to the top deck, gave them our blessings and set them free. They flew to one of the nearby lifeboats, ruffled their feathers in the warm sunshine, and began singing again. They had no intention of leaving the ship. So now they ride with us as stowaways.

They sleep in a fold of canvas stretched across the forward deck, just below the promenade deck. A sailor keeps them provided with fresh water, and almost all the passengers save food from their meals to throw down to them. They have become our best entertainers. Early each morning and late every afternoon they perch on rails or rigging and sing to appreciative audiences of humans. During the rest of the day they usually do flying acrobatics. They seem to be very proud of the fact that they can move through space so much faster and so much more gracefully than the humans watching them, the ship, the flying fish, the porpoises, the sharks, and even the sea birds.

As I watched them today, thinking of all the wise and helpful things birds can teach the rest of us, I was reminded of an extraordinary adventure I had one day in California with another little flying philosopher. For some time I had been in what we humans call a "low state of mind," due to an assortment of unpleasant experiences with other humans. I had lost faith in and respect for most of the people I knew. Nothing I did lifted me out of my discouragement and depression. One morning when I was at unusually low ebb, I left home and headed for the hills. It was the stormiest day of the year, raining in torrents, and to make the occasion complete, I started up the most barren and dismal canyon in that part of the country. It is dismal even on a sunny day.

Not far from the top of the canyon a sudden burst of melody stopped me short. It came from a mocking-bird, and he was standing on a swaying yucca stalk, flinging song recklessly in all directions. The canyon walls were echoing and re-echoing with the sound of him. I had never been interested in birds, and I wasn't interested in that particular bird. As a matter of fact, if he had fallen off and broken his neck it would probably have fitted my black mood better. The thing about him that stopped me was wondering how such volume of sound could come out of such a small throat. Then I got to speculating as to what he was doing out in such bad weather, when there were so many pleasant shelters for him to get under;

and why he should be so gay and happy when there was so little in the world about which to be gay and happy.

The harder it rained, the louder he sang. He refused to be drowned out. I decided that birds were subject to insanity just like humans. How long I stood there watching and listening to him I cannot tell you, but it was long enough for me to get wet through to my skin. Finally, he hit a high note and stopped abruptly. For a few seconds he aimed one of his eyes in my direction. Then he threw himself off his precarious perch, opened his wings, banked himself against the wind, circled past me, headed up the canyon, and disappeared over the ridge. That was the last I saw of him. But in those few flying seconds he taught me one of the most helpful lessons I ever learned. The essence of it I can condense into eleven words—HE NEVER LOOKED BACK TO SEE THE EFFECT OF HIS SONG.

Let me write it down again—HE NEVER LOOKED BACK TO SEE THE EFFECT OF HIS SONG. Isn't that something! The result on me was as immediate as it was revolutionary. It spun me around mentally and physically, and sent me down the canyon completely cured of my depression, without a care in the world and, actually singing. That bird had shown me what was wrong with my world. It wasn't the world that was to blame, or the people in it. It was I. My perspective had been warped. I had lost my sense of values. I had bogged myself by continuously looking back to see what others thought, or did not think, of MY "song," instead of giving what I had where I was, and then going on like that little fellow on the yucca stalk.

That bird was circulating outward with everything he had, giving of himself freely and generously. He was moving in the Cosmic order— from center to circumference. I had been trying to do the reverse, trying to make my circumference come into my center, to make everything circulate in towards me. And it wouldn't work that way. That bird was interested in outgo. I had been obsessed with income. He was moving at the best levels of himself. I had been crawling along my lower levels. He was living with ecstasy. I had been merely existing. He was not interested in creating an impression. Nor was he looking for personal rewards. Nor was he concerned over what I thought about his performance. He was merely being his part of the perfection of the universe, being it as best he knew how. He was speaking his own message in his own way, glorifying God in his own way. And because of this I was able through his eyes, his understanding, and his song, to find a better, more interesting, and more satisfying world to live in, despite the bad weather.

As I sloshed homeward something else exploded in my thinking areas; something which had a most significant connection with my experience with the mocking-bird; something which opened up all kinds of new vistas of relationships for me. Long ago a very uncommon individualist rode this spinning earth for awhile on a very uncommon mission. They called him Jesus of Nazareth, or Christ Jesus. Most of his time was devoted to liberating men and women from themselves, and helping them find and express their spiritual individualities in the common things of life. History has never recorded a greater authority on temporal and eternal life. Nor a wiser teacher. Nor a more successful healer of minds and bodies. Nor a more discerning and discriminating counsellor. Nor a finer gentleman. Nor a better neighbour. Nor one whose life and activities have been more respected; or more misunderstood and misrepresented.

He apparently realized that most of the men and women with whom he came in contact were not getting nearly as much out of life as they should, which he attributed to their inadequate and defective concepts of God, man, and the universe. So he went about among them in his friendly, sympathetic way, doing them good turns; and showing them how to improve their concepts and thereby their states of being. He was successful to an almost sensational degree. Not only did he show them how to make "the Kingdom of Heaven" a practical and continuing reality in their everyday lives; but he illustrated it by healing them of their physical, moral, and economic ills, and even lifting them out of the black illusion of death.

His dominion and control over materiality were amazing. So was his ability to make good prevail where evil had been prevalent and afflictive. People called him a miracle-worker, and attributed all kinds of weird and mysterious magical powers to him. But he told them that the unexpected and unbelievable good he was bringing

161

into their lives was not in the least miraculous, but the inevitable result of simple, natural spiritual laws. God's laws. Laws that were all-good, all·powerful, and irresistible. Laws that were ever-present and ever-available for every-one to use, providing his thinking and living moved in accord with the Laws.

Now one of his ingenious practices was to take some facet of this great, fundamental, spiritual Law moving through all existence, and tuck it inside some naïve parable, or folk tale, or bit of advice; and then leave it there without interpreta-tion or explanation for his hearers to dig out, if they cared to make the effort. He evidently wanted to make them use their individual thinking processes more than they were doing and to persuade them to be more childlike and God-trusting in their experiences with life. Upon one of these occasions, when the people were in much confusion and distress over social, political, and economic conditions, and apparently did not know which way to turn to solve these collective and individual problems, this unorthodox Teacher, with his far-reaching vision and ability to demon-strate whatever he said, advised them to go out and away from their own kind, and "behold the birds of the air," which, he pointed out, neither sowed, nor reaped, nor gathered into barns, and yet were abundantly taken care of by their heavenly Father.

If anyone followed his advice there seems to be record of it. I suppose it was difficult for them to get out beyond the cramped borders of the human species. Perhaps they did not believe wisdom and intelligence existed beyond the human species. Bird Beholders, in the sense the great Teacher must have meant, have apparently been few and far between in all centuries. The ages have produced many millions of experts in training, exhibiting, selling, shooting, cooking, and eating birds—but precious few Bird Beholders. Perhaps that is why the cycles of social, political, and economic disturbances have continued so uninterruptedly to this day. We weren't, it would appear, smart enough to follow one of the greatest tips in all history.

*I'll be seein' you*

# "CONSIDER THE LILIES"

*Kandy*
*Ceylon*

*To*

*Strongheart*
*Eternal Playground*
*Out Yonder*

Dear old Pal:

Kandy is a rapturous city in the mountains of Ceylon, a little over seventy miles from the equally rapturous coast city of Colombo. The ideal way to travel between them, if one has a fancy for adventure and stout legs, is to walk, sauntering along the main highway and stopping to explore every side road and interesting-looking trail. It is a vivid scenic show all the way, made up of jungle and rice-fields; rubber, tea, and pineapple plantations; villages of gay-colored houses, temples, and schools; throngs of people looking as though they had just stepped out of story-books; priests in yellow, red, and orange robes; water buffalos, bullocks, elephants, more elephants, and still more elephants. And ranges and degrees of smells that baffle description.

There were two things I particularly wanted to see here in Kandy—the place where most of the elephants are taken for their daily bath, and the botanical gardens. The visit to the bath was like attending a new kind of animal circus, a comedy circus; that to the botanical gardens, a pilgrimage into another world. The gardens cover approximately one hundred and fifty acres, and contain some of the finest and rarest trees, flowers, and plants in the world. A venerable native gardener with the most courtly manners, and an expert in his profession, acted as my guide and interpreter. As we walked slowly along he said an arresting thing in a most casual way. Sweeping his hands in all directions he whispered, as though afraid of disturbing the peaceful quietness of the place, "The trees and flowers are happy here. They get much love. So they grow well."

He greeted and spoke to trees, flowers, and plant quite as though they were human beings. And I know they talked back to him. He was a very wise man, a very advanced man. At the entrance to the spice gardens he left me to attend to some of his duties. I entered and found myself in a sniffer's paradise. The air was heavy and intoxicating with the mingled odors of clove, ginger, nutmeg, camphor, bay rum, lemon-grass, verbena, allspice, and other pungent things the names of which I do not know how to spell. Then I came to an enormous tree from India, the gift of a reigning rajah. Wondering how thick through it was at the base. I started to pace around it. On the far side I stumbled over a native who was sitting on the grass in front of some lilies in an old, rusty, tubular biscuit-tin. It was a stupid thing to do, but I had been watching the top of the tree instead of where I was placing my feet. I don't know which one of us was the more surprised.

He scrambled to his feet, bowed, and said something in a language I could not understand. I bowed. He bowed again. So did I. He was an old man as humans reckon time, but never have I seen a kindlier, happier, or more spiritualized face. He glowed like an old-fashioned lamp with plenty of good oil and a well-trimmed wick. He started to tell me something but I could not understand him. I listened carefully though, hoping in some way to get the drift of what he was trying to tell me. Finally I caught a word with which I was familiar: "Gurus" (teachers). And when he said it he was pointing at the lilies in the tin can. At that instant I knew I had found something rarer than anything else in the gardens. A Lily Considerer! A real Lily Considerer! Probably one of the few genuine specimens in existence!

And what a coincidence after my last letter, in which I told you about that extraordinary Teacher and Liberator of the First Century, Christ Jesus of Nazareth, and his advice to people about the birds. As I have already explained to you, this remarkable, but so little understood, man had such amazing dominion and control over time, space, material conditions, and even death that men and women were dumbfounded by his deeds, and especially by what they called his miracles. They thought of him as supernatural, but he assured them again and again that they not only could perform the same "miracles," but do even greater things, if they would but follow his simple instructions. Among these instructions was the unparalleled advice about "beholding," or consulting, the birds of the air and the fields, as a remedy for solving personal social, political, and economic problems.

But this great Master of Spiritual and Temporal Wisdom did not stop with recommending birds as rational and good counsellors for humans. He advocated flowers, too. One day, when his fellow-beings were unusually concerned about themselves, "conditions," and this-and-that, as humans generally are, he told them to stop worrying about their bodies, and their food and drink, and their clothes, and such things; he told them to go out and "consider" (that is, to look at attentively, study, ponder, meditate on, and pay due attention to as affecting one's conduct or course of action) the "lilies of the field." He counseled them to observe how the lilies grew, and to note that while they did no toiling or spinning, they were better arrayed than "even Solomon in all his glory."

There is no evidence to show that anyone followed his advice about the lilies, any more than they did about the birds. It was probably too unorthodox for them. They were evidently too mentally and spiritually lazy in their cramped little human shells to peck their way out and at least give it a trial. History would indicate that most of them put the "reverse English" on his advice, and instead of considering lilies, concentrated on considering Solomon in all his glory. Solomon was undoubtedly easier for them to consider. "Solomons in their glory" usually are. He had all the outward, the show-off things they were interested in—wealth, fame, power, attention! Solomon could scarcely escape being considered with all his theatrical splash, splurge, and splutter. He proclaimed himself like a circus calliope.

Lily considering demands a much more delicate and sensitive technique. It requires more humility . . . more consecrated effort . . . more mental independence . . . more daring . . . more courage . . . more originality . . . more sincerity . . . more discernment . . . more imagination . . . and more love. That explains why there have been so few Lily Considerers down through the centuries. And that is why my stumbling over that fragrant old native with his lilies was something in the nature of an historical event. I had never seen a real Lily Considerer before. I had heard humans talk about them in moments of religious emotion or sentiment, but I had never seen one of them actually functioning.

With his permission I sat on the grass with him. I would see what I could do as a Considerer. My bare-bodied friend tucked his feet under him, relaxed, placed his hands on his legs with palms upwards, half closed his eyes in the direction of the lilies, and mentally took off for parts unknown. I, too, narrowed my sight and interest to the lilies. The more I watched the more apparent it became that those lilies were not existing through any power of their own, but because they were reflecting a vaster Something; a Something which was giving them their life, symmetry, beauty, and fragrance; and taking care of them in superb fashion. What they were receiving and diffusing so abundantly, and with irresponsible ease, had a divine and an eternal flavor to it.

Suddenly, and this is somewhat difficult to describe, they stopped being "just flowers" in an old rusty can. Instead they became Ambassadors. Aristocratic, but democratic Ambassadors from a world of pure Spirit. Ambassadors from a God-made, God-managed country of pure delight. A country of utter loveliness . . . nobility . . . goodness . . . gladness . . . courtesy . . . tranquility . . . contentment . . . refinement . . . gentility . . . neighborliness . . . harmony . . . active good will . . . and immaculate law and order.

Only a handful of lilies bunched together intimately in an old rusty can! But they were doing something that the human species has been unable to achieve in all its centuries of development. They were maintaining flawless perfection in individual and group living. It wasn't difficult to understand why they were doing so much better in their group relationships than humans. They were using a better technique. It was a technique free from such defective human characteristics as selfishless . . . vanity . . . smugness . . . exclusiveness . . . insincerity . . . pretense . . . dishonesty . . . prejudice . . . indifference . . . apathy . . . intolerance . . . suspicion . . . bitterness . . . resentment . . . rivalry . . . greed . . . combativeness . . . malice . . . cruelty . . . tyranny . . . injustice . . . anxiety . . . fear . . . combative action . . . and the desire to possess, control, and dominate.

Each lily was giving its best, and only its best, in a happy, harmonious, group activity. In turn the group was contributing its best, and only its best, to what appeared to be an endless series of other individual and group harmonies, circulating out to infinite proportions. To the divine Totality of all Things, I guessed. What especially interested me was that while each lily was participating loyally in the group activity, each was maintaining its own individuality and uniqueness intact. There was no domination. No personal control. No interference. No friction. Each lily was thoroughly being its own self, but constructively and coöperatively. Each was unfolding in its own way and at its own tempo, without any prodding or condemnation from the others. Like that mocking-bird on the yucca stalk, each of them was sharing its particular gift with the universe, was speaking its own message in its own way, was glorifying God in its own way. And while that mocking-bird never looked back to see the effect of its song, those lilies never even glanced sideways to see what effect their beauty and fragrance were having on the life about them.

As I slipped quietly away so as not to disturb the meditations of my companion, I understood, I believe, why that wise Galilean had urged humans to "consider" lilies. I have tried it. And now I know, through that revealing and enlightening experience, that in the heart and the life of a lily lies the solution for every individual and collective human problem.

*I'll be seein' you*

# PLENITUDE

*Bombay*
*India*

*To*

*Strongheart*
*Eternal Playground*
*Out Yonder*

Dear old Pal:

Two of the world's most opposite types of rich men rubbed elbows on a busy street corner in downtown Bombay today while waiting for traffic signals to change, looked one another over casually, and were then lost in the crowd. One of them, an Occidental, was a fashion plate of smart tailoring and was accompanied by a secretary-bodyguard. The other, an Oriental, had on a coarse, homespun loin-cloth, a cloak of the same material, and was barefooted. The Occidental is rich in business enterprises, real estate, stocks, bonds, and money. The Oriental's only worldly possessions consist of a few sacred books, the things he wears, and some toilet articles which he carries with him in a large handkerchief. His wealth is entirely in spiritual values.

Two courageous and daring adventurers on life's high seas, both of them searching for the same ultimate objectives, but going after them in completely different ways. Being acquainted with them, I know that what each of them is really trying to attain is plenitude of being . . . the capacity to understand and be understood, to love and be loved . . . security . . . enlarged freedom, happiness and satisfaction . . . peace of mind and heart . . . perfection. The Occidental is trying to get them materially with almost complete disregard for the spiritual. The Oriental is striving for them spiritually with almost complete disregard for the material.

One is laying up treasure "on earth," the other "in heaven." One is interested in things without, the other in things within. One is working towards self, the other away from self. One is concerned with quantity, the other with quality. One is getting all he can, the other giving all he can. They are entirely unlike in motives and actions, and yet in their respective parts of the world each is admired for his "great wealth," each is considered a conspicuous example of success, and each has an important influence on the lives of thousands of his fellow-beings. They walk the same earth but live in totally different worlds.

In the Occidental's world he is a top-notcher. His is a world where life is based on a heartless, aggressive, ruthless, competitive system; where success is measured in terms of cash, power, and influence; and where stress is laid not on what is right or best, but on who wins. In that world few surpass him in political strategy and business warfare. He works entirely for personal interest and advantage—like a poker player. If it were possible he would fence off the earth and extract tribute from everyone on it. That would satisfy his ambitions admirably. And yet in his leisure hours, like his present tour of the world, he is delightfully companionable and most considerate in his realtionships with others.

In the Oriental's world he, too, is a top-notcher, even though his only assets are those within his thinking areas. His spiritual, social, moral, and political influence in India is enormous. People have the deepest respect and admiration for him. His interests are devoted to making the Golden Rule, a practical reality, and in sharing whatever good comes into his possession, as well as his services, with others. He is one of the most selfless men I have ever known, seems to have perpetual peace of mind, and is as independent of externals as a dog. Indeed, he is a very doglike human, which is high praise for any of my species. He has been accomplishing important results here in India for a long time, and he does most of it through the sheer force of his fine character and example. The material world with its physical lures and delights has no attraction for him. He is in quest of the Reality beyond his sense perceptions.

I wish it were possible to get these two unusual men into a quiet Bombay garden, and listen to them talk about life from their respective points of view. It would be an illuminating experience, to say the least; for while they would enjoy one another, they would be in almost complete disagreement on every subject they could discuss. Each of them, I know, would believe that the other was wasting his life chasing unrealities; and I doubt if either could be persuaded to retreat from his attitude. But they would stimulate one another, nevertheless, and each be the better for the experience. It would be nice to have you along at such a garden party. You would be the exception they could agree on, since both of them like dogs.

Having watched so many thousands of humans react to you, I know about what they would do when they saw you come bounding into a garden. What would be more interesting would be to see how you would react to them. My guess is that you would be polite but rather formal and offish with the Occidental; and turn on that "personality lure" of yours, and make the Oriental show you what games he knew how to play with four-legged friends. The Occidental raises dogs for show and commercial purposes. He would give close heed to your physical appearance, your pedigree, your record as a show and working dog, and the honors you have won. The fortune you earned as a movie actor would particularly impress him. Your inwardness rather than your outwardness would appeal to the Oriental. He would get the "feel" of those grand qualities of yours the moment he saw you. He is an authority on inner values; an authority, let me add, in a country where moral worth is rated as wealth, and material wealth as a fleeting illusion.

And speaking of these things, lend your ear to this! Your success and popularity were due to the way that man Trimble helped you to develop those splendid, latent qualities of yours and get them into expression. They were not "freak" qualities, as so many believed, but qualities

174

possessed by every dog; qualities that have endeared dogs to humans ever since dogs and humans first began walking the earth together. In all parts of India today, millions of devout men and women are striving, through prayer, discipline, and sacrifice, to attain and maintain in their lives these very dog qualities. And I say this with the deepest respect. Whenever I ask an Indian what qualities he is trying to incorporate into his own mind, heart, and activities, he invariably mentions the qualities we humans admire so much in you dogs.

I suppose they would be startled and shocked if I pointed out to them how well, how consistently and how easily you dogs express so much of the "superior inwardness" they themselves are striving for. But that would not be true about the Oriental I have already mentioned. He knows what fine, uplifting things you dogs have to share with humans. But then he is a very exceptional human. He bases his thinking and actions on the conviction that he is in, and a functioning part of, a universe that is alive with God. Therefore, he searches for manifestations of God in everything—Nature, humans, dogs, birds, wild animals, insects, snakes, and even forms of life that most people would regard as repellent. He believes that the Creator-intelligence speaks through everything that exists, to those who have eyes to see, ears to hear, and hearts to understand.

The attempt on the part of humans to break up life into such groupings as higher and lower . . . good and bad . . . important and unimportant . . . essential and unessential, he regards as one of its greatest futilities and sins. His attitude about it is that if God's presence is anywhere, it must be everywhere. And that if God's presence is everywhere, then everything is part of the divine plan and perfection, however contradictory and distorted this may seem to the physical senses. The imperative need at the moment, he says, is for man to get back to, and understand, his God-source as quickly as possible, and learn how to move out with it. This he believes is an individual rather than a group activity, and begins with self-purification and self-consecration. Through purification comes reverence for all life, he says. Through reverence for all life comes response. Through response comes coöperation. Through coöperation comes coördination. Through coördination come right relationships. And through right relationships comes the ultimate Perfection.

*I'll be seein' you*

## PLAY

*To*

*Strongheart*
*Eternal Playground*
*Out Yonder*

Dear old Pal :

Egypt is an old stamping ground of mine, so being here is not a new experience. It is a country I am exceedingly fond of exploring, especially by caravan. You would not like it here, though. It is much too flat, sandy, and hot for your tastes.

I left the ship at Suez and came over the eighty miles of desert in an automobile, piloted by a stout, potato-faced Arab with phenomenally high notions as to the rate of speed at which humans should move through space when they do not have to make the exertion themselves. He was able to drive at dizzy speeds, he assured me, because Allah was always with him. It was a fantastic trip all the way from Suez to Cairo, in which villages, Bedouin camps, caravans, camels, donkeys, dogs, and the upness and downess of desert appeared and disappeared in the most absurd manner. The country was all right. It was the curves and the bumps and the skids which broke the scenic continuity for me. But we reached Cairo intact, which, all things considered, is something to brag about. One of the most fascinating ways to make this journey is to get a guide and a couple of running dromedaries, not pack camels, and follow one of the old caravan routes from city to city. In this way one gets to really know the country and is able to blend himself with its peculiar moods and rhythms.

Most people come to Egypt to see and study the ruins of ancient civilizations, or to amuse themselves in Cairo, which has long been an international social playground. Play styles here differ from season to season, as they do in most of the other places where cosmopolitan society gathers to strut itself. But while this is a play city, I doubt if any of you dogs would recognize as play what goes on in the social zones. It is too studied, too formal, too artificial, and too circumscribed. A dog would probably wonder why men and women, presumed to be such superior specimens of organic existence, worked so hard to have a good time and seemed to be getting so little real happiness and fun out of it. If he started reasoning it out from his own point of view, the dog would undoubtedly conclude that what was needed in these society activities was less humanness and more dogness. That is, more naturalness . . . more sincerity . . . more spontaneity . . . more genuine play spirit . . . more enthusiasm . . . more ecstasy of living . . . more freedom of action . . . and more companionability.

Many humans would agree with such dog conclusions, for it is no secret that something has been seriously wrong with our senses of relationships and play for a long time. We do not get along well with one another, and we do not play well together. All species seem to begin their earth experiences with attractive and flexible capacities for relating themselves happily to the world about them and having lots of fun with anything and everything. Look at puppies, for instance! Or kittens! Or colts! Or baby lambs and goats, with a touch of Spring in the air! Or any of those other forms of new life appearing! There is companionship for you! And play! And excitement! And amusement! And satisfying experience! And how simple, and natural, and spontaneous it is in its coördination!

I wish I were expansive and wise enough to be able to see life from a dog's point of view. I would like to find out scientifically how it is that you dogs manage to carry the spirit of good fellowship and play throughout your earth experience? How you manage to have as much sparkling fun when "full grown" as when you are puppies? It would be worth a great deal to any human really to know this. We humans usually have our best fun when we are children. We get some of our clearest views of reality then, only we never know it at the time. As children we appear to others to be living on a material earth under the ownership-control of older relatives. Actually though, we do not live on the earth at all, but in an entirely different world. Worlds, in fact! Worlds of our own creation. Worlds filled with all sorts of delightful and fascinating things. Worlds we can make appear and disappear at will. Worlds we can manage without assistance from those ever-dominating relatives.

The most precious contacts we have in these worlds are the fairy folk, or thought-people. Sometimes they come alone, sometimes in countless numbers—depending upon what has to be done. They go with us on our mental journeys. They companion us in our mental adventures. And what friends and pals they are! They cannot be seen by human eyes; that is why they are able to troop by our directing relatives so successfully. They can only be seen mentally or spiritually. It is difficult to describe these fairy folk, or thought-people, as they refuse to stay inside human descriptions. If you try to bind a definition around them, they pop out of it and make faces at you. But I can tell you this much about them: they are wise, loving, considerate, understanding, fun-loving, given to harmless pranks, and are very effective in action, especially when one is confronted by the bogeyman of evil. As we grow older we often speak of these fairy folk, or thought-people, as ideas. Some prefer calling them angel visitants.

Elders often look askance at their children's magic worlds and thought-playmates, and call them childish, time-wasting, silly, and even injurious. They cannot get into them, you see, and boss things around. So they do not approve of them. But these attitudes are changing fast, and for a very startling reason. The modern scientists, who have been exploring far and wide, are kicking the material world out from under us. Or rather they are dissolving it from under us by declaring the whole thing immaterial and illusory.

But they do not stop there. They have been sending word back to the rest of us for some time to the effect that the more they investigate, the more apparent it becomes that the so-called fanciful, make-believe words of children, poets, artists, sages, and saints are actually nearer the reality of existence than that which humans have all along been thinking they were seeing and experiencing as a material universe. Which, let me add, has been playing havoc with our traditional intellectual routines.

The most tragic occasion in every little human's life is that day when his elders compel him to set aside his "worlds of make-believe," and begin preparing to take his place in the "struggle" or "battle for existence." It means a revolutionary change in his outlook and behavior patterns, particularly those having to do with relationships and play. In most instances it means saying good-bye to the fairy folk, or thought-companions of so many happy hours, and substituting "hard, practical facts" approved by unimaginative elders. Many youngsters protest and rebel, but it does no good. The elders have majority opinion and the stronger muscles on their side. This transitional period is usually as bitter as it is confusing. Behind the little fellow are the playgrounds of frolicsome, carefree Togetherness. Ahead, he is warned, are series upon series of social, economic, political, religious, and military battlefields upon which, he is being taught, he must either conquer his fellows or be conquered by them. For the sake of security and advantage he is persuaded to join one or more human packs, in which he willingly submerges his individuality and runs to order with them.

All of which helps to explain why humans are in such continuous warfare. We have educated ourselves out of the art of being companionable; consequently we do not play well together, or do much of anything else well together. We could learn much to our advantage from you dogs in these matters. For instance, you dogs fling everything you have into your relationships. You insist upon putting the spirit of play into everything you do, and making whatever it is yield rich dividends in satisfaction not only for yourselves but for all concerned. In your sense of play there are no conflicting interests, no competitive action, no straining after results, no rewards, no victories, and no defeats. Just "oddity, frolic, and fun," with each contributing the best he has, and all sharing alike.

The average young human begins his earth-ride with a delightful, doglike sense of play, but this changes as he grows older and begins imitating other humans. For the fragrant Togetherness he substitutes division, personal ambition, rivalry, acquisitiveness, opposition, and conflict. Instead of sharing of himself freely and generously with his fellows, he wants to compete with them. He wants to fight them. He wants a miniature war. He becomes ambitious to beat somebody at something for something; to vanquish a foe; to demonstrate superiority; to be admired; to be idolized; to collect "spoils" in the form of applause, reputation, career, titles, trophies, and money.

The storm signals about this have been up for some time, but we pay little attention to them. The spiritual experts watching and appraising the world scene say that we humans are headed for inevitable doom, unless we purge the selfishness and militancy from our minds and hearts, and learn to get along with our fellow-beings in a neighborly way. One of the most effective ways to accomplish this, they believe, is for each human to recapture his child-heart and get the spirit of genuine play and fun back into his everyday living again. If the human can relearn how to play *with* others instead of *against* them, they say, he can relearn how to do everything else *with* others instead of *against* them. Which sounds like unusually good sense, doesn't it?

*I'll be seein' you*

# CONCEALED WEAPONS

*Venice*
*Italy*

*To*

*Strongheart*
*Eternal Playground*
*Out Yonder*

Dear old Pal:

I am now in Italy—to be specific, Venice. You might not be interested in what we humans regard as the historical loveliness of this famous old city, but you would like the beaches, the canals, and, in a very big way, the gondolas. Boats, to you! The gondolas are much more fun to ride in than automobiles. They move with greater smoothness, and there is enough uncertainty about them to make every ride sporty. I never get into one without wondering what you would be like riding on the forward deck. You would certainly be a show for the populace, if you behaved as strenuously as you usually did when we went motoring. That you would bark yourself overboard in your excitement is a certainty, but that wouldn't bother you in the least with your fondness for adventure and swimming.

Venice is one of the "front gateways" into Italy. Visitors are always detained here long enough for inspectors to examine them and their baggage, to determine their fitness, or lack of fitness, for entering the country. After I got past the official scrutiny this morning, I went to watch a ship astern of ours unload immigrants. They came down the gangway not like individuals with participating rights in the human family, but prodded along like cattle. Their faces bore mute testimony to an over-abundance of bad treatment, injustice, hardships, and suffering. Many of them were obviously seething inwardly against the existing social and economic order, but not enough to erupt outwardly. Perhaps they lacked only leadership!

As they stepped ashore a small army of uniformed men herded them into a kind of corral and began searching and ticketing them. The inspectors were looking particularly for knives, guns, bombs, and other forms of deadly weapons, which may not be brought into the country. They did a thorough job of it, but I did not see any of them find any weapons. And yet I know that man after man went through that probe and entered Italy "armed to the teeth." Those immigrants were not carrying weapons concealed on their persons or in their baggage; they had them tucked away in their thinking, a place government officials rarely search. Once inside the country, and away from prying eyes, they would have little difficulty in transforming those concealed mental weapons into physical ones, and carrying out whatever purposes they had in mind.

That smuggling through of mental armament would not have attracted my attention if I had not learned what I did from you about listening to the mental qualities, and watching the mental attitudes in my vicinity. I do not profess to do this as well as you, or many other four-legged animals I know, but I am better at it than I was when I had only human training to go on. You would never have permitted the kind of inward hostility that many of those immigrants were carrying to have come near you without doing something corrective about it. You would have sensed that lurking animosity even before the human casings for it came into physical view. You would have picked it out of the surrounding atmosphere it was polluting. Then knowing what was first mentally and then physically moving in your direction, you would have been ready for it. And that, old Pal, is more than any of those inspectors could have done with all their training and experience.

As you must have observed, the human pays relatively little attention to his own thinking processes, or to the thought atmosphere about him. Theoretically, at least, he knows he should; for he is aware that good and bad thought attitudes, when set in motion, always come back to him again, bringing accumulated good for the good set in motion, and accumulated bad for the bad. He knows, in some degree, that these things work with the precision and accuracy of law; that they are, in fact, law. But in his everyday contacts with his fellow-men, he sets aside the mental qualities and appraises them by externals; by financial standing, social position, physical appearance, clothes and, compliance with the prevailing conventions and loyalties.

What the other fellow may be doing in his thinking seldom interests the human, unless it becomes too objectionable or threatening in outward expression. That is why so many humans are brought low by mental weapons, without ever understanding what hit them. As I have told you before, the human is probably the only species on earth that tries to be outwardly social and inwardly antisocial, at one and the same time. But he gets away with it best only among his own species. When he attempts it with the four-legged animals he usually runs into difficulties sooner or later. They read his mind and intentions too well.

No one seemed to be the least interested in what those immigrants were thinking about today; no one wanted to learn, for instance, what they had hidden in their secret hopes, wishes, longings, desires, inclinations, and ambitions. The inspectors searched only clothes and baggage, and then permitted their owners to enter the country with official approval. But of this I am sure: if by some modern necromancy, the thinking of those immigrants could have been broadcast over a nation-wide radio hook-up, someone in authority would have ordered out all branches of the army, and perhaps even the navy.

One of these days we humans will probably be compelled by bitter experience to do something about the undisciplined, unsocial, and destructive thinking skulking back of camouflaged, respectable exteriors. When that time comes I believe countries will protect themselves by establishing mental quarantine stations on their frontiers, where every human's thinking will be exhaustively examined and tested by experts, before he is permitted to enter. Imagine what might happen to the world if each country set up strict quarantine against such corroding mental poisons as ill will . . . prejudice . . . intolerance . . . suspicion . . . hatred . . . deceit . . . selfishness . . . dishonesty . . . covetousness . . . combativeness . . . bad manners . . . greed . . . jealousy . . . envy . . . gossip . . . and slander!

With such strict regulations, I wonder how many of us humans would have enough of the right kind of inwardness to take us across the nearest foreign border; that is, without having to have our thinking fumigated! Now, there is something to give consideration to when I have more time. I wouldn't dare risk a guess on it at the moment, not with what I have been observing among my own species. But of this I am certain: you dogs would experience no difficulties at all getting through such mental controls, with your inner integrities and universal loyalties.

Watching those immigrants today, it occurred to me that someone was permitting a great deal of valuable human material to go to waste. True, they were a hard, sullen-looking lot, without much on their surfaces to recommend them; nevertheless, each one of them was a definite part of the great process of Life, and was entitled to be treated as such. Somewhere in each one of them, in spite of all that debris of human experience, was the eternal, divine Spark, that Spark which gives to each created thing its life, uniqueness, capacities, and the right to be and express itself in its own way. Because of this, and because of the immutable law of Individuality and Variety, through which the Cosmos functions as a unified Totality, it is natural to assume that every one of those immigrants had some particular gift, some particular talent, some particular mission, which he and he alone could perform for the glory of his Creator and the good of his fellow-men.

What those immigrants seemed to need more than anything else was a gentle hand extended in their direction; a hand moved by neighborly understanding; a hand that knew how to fan those divine sparks into flame; a hand that would help them by easy stages, even as Larry Trimble helped you, to bring the finer but unused areas of themselves into action and usefulness. What a valuable government investment that would be! But I doubt if the inspectors were equipped for such superior and delicate work. They were using the old, antiquated method of treating immigrants as similar things, rather than as individuals. Hence the human wastage.

*I'll be seein' you*

# ROOSTERS

*Paris*
*France*

*To*

*Strongheart*
*Eternal Playground*
*Out Yonder*

Dear old Pal:

The funniest thing I ever saw in connection
with you was that overdecorated, vainglorious,
rubber rooster that someone once sent you from
Paris. Remember him, and the riots he used to
cause in our little house after he had been in-
flated and placed in the middle of the floor?
What a rare bird he was! An impossible bird,
really! It still puzzles me how anyone arrived at
the decision to send a big police dog like you a
rubber rooster. He must have known by experience what rubber roosters usually do to police
dogs. I wish I knew who he was and where he
was, that I might thank him for all the entertainment he brought into our lives.

Let us fuse memories for a few minutes, while I
wave my magic wand and throw time into reverse.
The scene is the living-room of our Hollywood
house, on a pleasant autumn afternoon. I am sitting on the floor, and you are spread out near one
of the doorways, where you can watch all
entrances and keep a blinking eye on me. I am

examining a bright-colored pulpy thing in my hands, which does not interest you at all. At least it doesn't until I start blowing into it through a small tube. You open one eye a trifle. I continue to blow. You open both eyes. The blowing continues. You raise your head and stare. Things are happening between my face and hands. You get to your feet. You come closer. Your eyes are bulging, for in my hands there has suddenly appeared a full-sized rooster, undoubtedly the most garish-looking rooster that ever had breath blown into it.

I place him on the floor. Your ears go up like a mule's, your nose starts twitching, the hair on the back of your neck rises—always a sign you are "clearing ship for action." You cannot decide just what the thing is, or what it is doing there, or what its intentions are towards you. The air currents in the room start him swaying and jerking, giving him the appearance of being very much alive. You stretch cautiously forward and sniff. And when you sniff, you sniff! Your outgoing breath bends him backward. You intake pulls him forward. As he does so his crimson-and-yellow beak pops you on the tip of your nose. It isn't much of a blow, but enough to startle the wits out of you. You leap sideways and skid with a rug. Over goes the floor lamp, over goes a chair with books on it. That startles you even more. Pandemonium breaks loose!

You race around the room as though you had gone mad, knocking things over or out of place, filling the neighbourhood with the sound of your barking, and charging in and jumping away from that rooster as though he were giving you the toughest battle of your fighting career. I am holding my sides with laughter. I have never witnessed a more comical show. I am hoping you will jab one of those long fangs of yours into him. I want to see what will happen to all of us when he explodes. But you are too smart. You are only pretending to annihilate him as he rocks back and forth, wagging that empty head of his and defying you to come in closer and get another smack on the nose.

Then a very embarrassing thing happens, embarrassing for us but doubly so for him. Our cocky guest starts leaking. First, a crease appears across his multicolored back. Then, his rainbow-flecked chest becomes soft and flabby. The brilliantly colored tail droops. His rear end oscillates this way and that way, as though he wants to sit down but doesn't know how to manage it. His proud head bends neckward, as if he is ashamed of what is happening to him. He lurches drunkenly. His legs sag. He falls forward on his beak. There is a slight shudder. All that remains of the splendor of him is a pinch of rubber.

Where that rooster came from, and where he went to, interested you in the extreme, didn't it! Wasn't he the proud, self-centered thing! And didn't he enjoy showing off! Puffed full he was a perfect symbol of vanity at its peak. But he could never stay at peak. That was his secret tragedy. No matter how generous I was in sharing my breath with him, he could contain it for only a certain length of time. Then the leaking would begin and down he would droop into oblivion.

When his days finally came to an end, I tried to find another rooster like him for you, but without success.

Now I wave my magic wand again, and return us to Paris. This morning when I stepped out of my hotel a breath-taking sight greeted me. There on the sidewalk were a dozen or more rubber roosters so much like the one sent to you that they must have been cousins. The vendor who had them for sale had filled them with his breath, and placed them in a line on the sidewalk, like soldiers. There they stood, the puffed-up things, swaying conceitedly in the breeze as though demanding tributes of admiration from all passers-by. They were having their moments, but only their moments. All of them were afflicted with the malady common to all rubber roosters—breath leakage. The vendor would blow into them as much breath as they could contain, but after awhile it would start percolating through their rubber bodies in the usual distressing way, and down they would go into the nothingness whence they came.

Every human who came along stopped for a look and a laugh. At one time there were just as many humans looking at the roosters as there were roosters looking at the humans. It was a laughable scene. As I watched it, I wondered what a visitor from another planet, not familiar with us and our ways, would have thought if he too had been looking on. My conclusions were that he would have found the humans funnier than the rubber roosters. I'll tell you why. That particular boulevard is famous as a parade ground for human peacockery. It is one of the favored out-door places in Paris for displaying oneself, and pretending to be what one would like to be. Men and women strut there day and night in carefully studied and rehearsed efforts to impress others. They are supposed to be the last word in what men and women should look like and behave like in the presence of their fellows.

They were interesting to watch, of course, but the smartest and most attractive thing with breath in it that I saw along the boulevard was a German shepherd dog about your size. I am not trying to belittle my own species, but honesty compels me to say that that dog was topping every human—man or woman. Not one of those fashion-competing humans could have beaten, or even equaled, that dog in an all-species show; especially in such comparative tests as all-round excellence in species and type . . . natural attractiveness . . . posture . . . poise . . . coördina-tion . . . flexibility . . . carriage . . . rhythm . . . demeanor . . . universality of appeal . . . spirit . . . individuality . . . self-confidence . . . self-respect . . . and style of going. The humans may have had the clothes lines, but the dog had the body lines.

That dog, without the least effort to do so, was creating continuous interest as he walked along the boulevard. People looked at him admiringly and affectionately, then turned and looked at him again. He was irresistible, but then he was almost flawless in appearance and move-ment. The humans on parade were not doing nearly so well, even though they were using all the known techniques and tricks to attract favorable attention to themselves. By Parisian standards they were doing an excellent job, but they could have done much better with some of that dog's inner equipment. He could have taught them, providing, of course, they had the receptivity, that real value, real worth, and even real authority are not matters of outward display and proclamation, but come from the radiation of fine qualities of mind and heart.

We humans, it is true, have an inherent tendency to inflate ourselves like rubber roosters, and become conceited, pretentious, affected, self-centered, insincere, artificial, and pharisaically smug. But in spite of this, there is deep down in every one of us an abiding admiration and respect for all that is genuinely and unobtrusively good. And that, let me add, is why by simply being yourselves, you dogs are able to do so much for the members of the human species.

*I'll be seein' you*

## EYES FOR THE BLIND

*London*
*England*

*To*

*Strongheart*
*Eternal Playground*
*Out Yonder*

Dear old Pal:

Since arriving in England there have been so many things to do that there has scarcely been time to sleep, to say nothing of letter-writing. But today things are different. I am on a train that is just leaving London for Plymouth, where I am to take a boat for the United States. It is an ideal time for writing, for fog has obliterated the landscape, and all the people I should like to talk with are either settling down for "forty winks" or have their noses aimed into books. So I make a belated report to you.

Let me begin by saying that while to most people you are now only kennel and motion-picture history, something of you akin to the famous soil of John Brown, that great individualist of American civil war days, still goes marching on, and turning up in the most unexpected places and at the most unexpected times. Until you sky-rocketed into fame as the star of "The Silent Call," few people had ever before seen in action a dog of your size, power, intelligence, and all-round accomplishments. They regarded you as a super-dog, and by way of tribute spoke of you as the "almost human dog," which was supposed to be a flattering honor for you and a sort of left-handed tribute to themselves.

Having been accustomed to regarding dogs as more or less unimportant biological objects that were dependent on the human for what little intelligence and usefulness they had, they were not prepared for you. So when you burst upon them as a top-bracketed, dramatic, box-office attraction, you sent them, at least temporarily, into a collective daze. They did not know that those "amazing capacities" of yours were latent in every dog, merely needing perception and co-öperation to be brought into expression. They preferred thinking of you as an unusually gifted animal, trained to unusual perfection.

Few of them realized how well you had been educated, even in the human sense of that term; or suspected for a moment that you were doing many of those so-called feats of yours absolutely on your own without direction. Wouldn't they have been surprised if they had known that your tutor, as well as all other humans associated with you, had been in the habit of treating you as an independent rational unit, with unlimited capacities for independent thinking . . . for grasping the meaning of things . . . for communicating and exchanging ideas . . . for improvement and development . . . and for coöperative activity with them!

Most of your film fans liked best to watch you trail after villains and fight them. No one could ever sit calmly in his theater chair while that was going on. And what a mean, vicious, cruel, dirty lot those villains were! The producers made them that way on purpose. It always worked up a greater emotional and dramatic thrill when you started after them. Your fight climaxes, usually on high cliffs, were always sensational entertainment—even for your cameramen. But I wonder what audiences would have thought if they had known that all those "terrific battles" were only play-times for you and the actors. True, you always tore their clothes to shreds, occasionally leaving them quite naked, but let this be proclaimed: in all those strenuous fight scenes you were never known to leave the mark of fang or nail on any actor's body. You certainly knew your stuff!

I wish that all those fans of yours could have seen you when you were not playing like that, when you were really doing police work and really trailing down a real bad man. Then they would have seen something to remember, especially if the bad man tried to resist you with a gun, club, or knife! Your police work was worth going a long way to see. Personally, though, I preferred watching you serve as eyes for the blind, or as a "nursemaid" to children. You always seemed to be at your best then, probably because their need of you brought out the best in you. You are the first dog I ever saw act as eyes for the blind. How you could snake them through traffic and in and out of buildings! They needed no preliminary training with you, did they! All they had to do was to hang on to that short leash, talk to you as they would to another human, and leave the rest to you.

The example you set in this form of service through the medium of your pictures is achieving splendid results, as schools for training dogs for this work have been established all over the world. In most of them the humans undergo as much training as the dogs. An excellent idea, too. Studying together, the human and the dog learn to function as a unit, and usually they develop such great mutual understanding that it overflows into the divine. I believe that the next forward step in man-dog unit development will be in using dogs as companion-guides for humans who have gone morally blind.

For your personal information, moral blindness is raising havoc among the human species. Experts regard it as far worse for the individual and the community than physical blindness. It generally begins with some kind of a seemingly unimportant mental and moral defect that spreads across the victim's vision, blurring and distorting it, which causes him to drop to lower levels of himself. One of the definite symptoms of this moral blindness is evident when a human could have done better in some aspect of his life, but fails to do so. It is an affliction peculiar to the human species.

Now let me recall something to your memory that has a direct bearing on what I am saying. One day when you and I were keeping house together in the hills of Hollywood, two men came to see you, both of them enthusiastic fans of yours. One was white; the other, black. The white man was an important figure in big business and politics, and had much wealth. The black man was his servant, with years of service back of him. The white man was disappointed when he learned that I had had nothing to do with your training. He wanted some firsthand pointers about you for use with dogs he was breeding for show purposes. I told him I thought the best plan was for him to discuss the matter with you. So we three went out to find you. Then the climax! Or rather, the anti-climax! You chased him back into the house. Remember! And then, to make matters worse for both of us, you deliberately went over to the black man with your tail wagging in the friendliest way, encouraged him to pat your head and sides, and gave out the impression that you liked him better than anyone you had met in a long time. Remember how annoyed the white man was when he left! But so were you. And that made it "even Stephen."

At the time, I thought you were very wrong in your attitude and bad mannered. And I told you so. But now I have to take it all back, for the intervening years have confirmed the accuracy of your judgment of him. He fooled me completely. He fooled millions of other humans, too, with his attractive personality, the glamor of his successes, and the way he dramatized himself. But he could not fool you. You did something that countless thousands now wish they had been able to do themselves. You read him and his motives aright on sight. Although it was a long time making the discovery, the world now knows that back of that mask of respectability and that social veneer stalked a cunning, unprincipled, ruthless, acquisitive, lawless, self-intoxicated human marauder. He was simply a slick, dressed-up bandit. A menace to society. An enemy of civilization. A traitor to the universe of which he was a part. He had no regard for anyone's welfare but his own. You met him at his peak, when he had conquered almost everything, except himself.

He could have done great things for the world with his exceptional talents, but he was too much interested in himself. Like so many other opportunists with anti-social tendencies, great wealth, power, influence, and a knowledge of the weaknesses of human nature, he became highly proficient in "handling" public officials, and getting around laws—that is, man-made laws. Then one day the inevitable happened. He ran head-on into laws he could not manipulate—the inflexible, exacting laws of a moral universe. And they not only knocked him for the proverbial loop, but rolled him out flat.

Today I crossed the trail of what is left of him. He is living in a tiny place just outside London. The wealth is gone, and so is the influence, the power, and most of his health. Everyone deserted him except the colored man who came with him that day in Hollywood, and who now pushes him around in a wheel chair. Those "mills of God" certainly grind "exceeding small" when they grind!

The white man's financial crash was bad, but his spiritual crash was worse. It happened while he was in England. The black man pulled him out of the general wreckage, found the little house, and moved him into it. Then he did a Solomon-like thing. He went to an animal refuge, begged a dog, and brought it home for his almost helpless master. It wasn't much of a dog from a show-man's point of view, but it had an abundance of vitality, enthusiasm, and affection, an irrepress-ible sense of humor, and a great capacity for non-critical companionship. The dog and the man adopted each other at sight.

That happened some months ago. Since then a miracle has been taking place, for, out of that almost hopeless human wreckage, a new man is emerging. Slowly and rather timidly, to be sure, but he is emerging. And that dog is the cause of it. He began by being so entertaining and amusing that the man in the wheel chair had to watch him. Then he lured the man into playing with him, and the more they played, the more the man moved out of his morbid introspection and suicidal depressions. Then, almost without the man being aware of it, the dog began uncovering in him long-buried treasures of faith, hope, and affection; teaching him how to let the best of himself get out, and really care; and illustrating for him in easy lessons what great possibilities life has to offer when one is wise enough to keep it simple, genuine, unselfish and fragrant.

Yes, it is a miracle; the miracle of a little tramp dog leading a human out of moral blindness.

*I'll be seein' you*

# FINGER-WAGGING

*Atlantic Ocean*

*To*

*Strongheart*
*Eternal Playground*
*Out Yonder*

Dear old Pal:

"Europe has gone to the dogs! The United
States is going there too unless, and I quote, 'all
the red-blooded, two-fisted, patriotic he-men get
together at once and do something about it!' "
That catastrophic information reached us less than
an hour ago via radio, coming across miles o
boisterous ocean from an equally boisterous ban-
quet in New York. The speaker who shouted this
dire prediction, as he considered it, was a well
known politician with a gift for dramatizing himself; and he was erupting like a volcano, flinging
sound and fury in all directions. He seemed to be
annoyed at every country in the world, except the
United States; and at everyone in the United
States except himself, with whom he appeared to
be going over in a big way.

As radio entertainment he was sub-zero. He
had a loud, well-trained voice and an extensive
vocabulary of imposing words, but almost no
ability for saying anything worth remembering.
He was foam without substance, but at that his
foam was potent enough to travel across all the

watery space between us and the coast-line of the United States, and to penetrate a noisy nor'easter which has been knocking our ship around for the past three days. I was walking out of his vocal range, with feet wide apart because we were rolling and pitching heavily, when I heard that hackneyed phrase about "going to the dogs." And I sizzled more than I have in a long time.

Why humans use this phrase in the insolent way they do baffles me. It is so unoriginal. So thoughtless. So stupid. So undeserved. Even the most illiterate human ought to know better, for even the most illiterate knows from personal observation what exceptionally high averages in character and conduct the average dog maintains throughout his earthly experience. Knows, too, the richness of the dog in such admirable assets as personal integrity . . . unselfed service . . . loyalty . . . devotion . . . sincerity . . . honesty . . . constancy . . . courage . . . and trustworthiness. Most of us humans gladly admit that we like and admire dogs for their fine qualities, and their stimulating companionships; and yet when we want to hang a really degrading indictment on a fellow-being, we say he is "going to the dogs." That is about as low as we can shove him.

Now anyone who has grasped something of the true dimensions and purposes of a dog, and is averagely familiar with human history, will agree that it would have been better for all concerned if humanity had started going to the dogs centuries ago, not as a mark of disgrace, but to learn from them some of the essentials for riding the earth sanely and happily which dogs know so well. As self-elected, top specimens of organic life, we humans believe we know how to ride the earth sanely and happily, but the fact seems to be that no other species mismanages its affairs quite as badly. The human record, particularly that part having to do with our conduct toward one another, is shocking beyond anything you or any other dog could possibly understand. And yet when we spot a worse than average defective among us, we elevate our noses, generally clasped by thumb and finger, and arrogantly announce that he is "going to the dogs."

What that politician howled into the radio in New York tonight is of no great importance. He always blows off like that when he gets an opportunity. Only I wish he hadn't said it, as it is such a cowardly libel on dogs. He is what is known as a professional finger-wagger. Ever hear of that term? If you haven't, let me tell you that finger-wagging is of the nature of a malady and is peculiar to the human species. It usually develops from self-magnification. Or an uncontrolled ambition for imparting information. Or a craving for converting, regulating, and dominating others. Or a passion for making the world conform to one's personal beliefs and notions about things. Or all of them combined. Now when the human sets his tongue to wagging, he has a habit of stiffening one of his index fingers and wagging it in rhythm with his tongue as an instrument of authority. Hence—finger-wagging.

When we humans are young our parents finger-wag us almost continuously, telling us what we may and may not do. Then various kinds of teachers go to work on us, with relatives and friends finger-wagging us on the side, unless by chance we beat them to it and do the finger-wagging ourselves. In its milder forms, finger-wagging is harmless and often amusing. But in its more advanced stages, it has a tendency to become extremely self-centred, abnormal, fanatical, dictatorial, tyrannical, dangerous and destructive.

That politician belonged to the blatant, or the blah-blah type of finger-wagger. He makes his living wagging his finger at people and vocally stirring up their emotions, sentiments and prejudices in order to get them to react favorably to whatever promotional scheme he is interested in at the moment. There was nothing modest about his evaluation of himself. He was, he announced, speaking for "the people of the United States." Politicians have a way of spreading themselves like that. But while he was speaking for them, he was sending millions of them to "the dogs" because of their backwardness in thinking and moving in unison with him. He probably did not know that he was proclaiming his own imperfections louder than all the faults he was condemning in others. He was proclaiming them in his manners, the tone of his voice, the things he said, and the way he said them. Like all finger-waggers, he found it easier to point out the blemishes in others, than to get rid of his own. Inferiority always acts like that, they say. It seeks to cover its own defects by uncovering those of others.

Everyone aboard this ship has the malady. From early morn to late at night, from the top to the lowest deck, wherever humans meet, it is chatter-chatter-chatter! Talk-talk-talk! Gabble-gabble-gabble! Opinions, information, advice, judgments, rulings, warnings, instructions, predictions, gossip and general hocus-pocus flow almost without interruption from mouths to ears. People talk whether they have anything worth saying or not. The trick is to find someone who will really listen. Everyone wants to do the talking, to be the teacher, the dictator. Apparently no one has heard that "the worthwhile and enduring things of life are generated only in active silence."

Some say that all this excessive and needless talking is merely the exhaust from running our mental and emotional engines too fast, and that it is harmless unless inhaled in large quantities. Others insist that it is due entirely to our fear that those with whom we come in contact will not recognize the degree of importance we have conferred upon ourselves. But whatever its real cause, the experts in tabulating the human scene agree that most of our individual and collective difficulties come from talking too much, and assuming too great a responsibility for the conduct of others. What we humans need, they say, are fewer finger-waggers and more doers. Less teaching and preaching, and more practice. Fewer theorists and theories, and more good examples.

On the surface that looks like a difficult thing to bring about. But I know how a good start could be made. Get every nation to hold a NATIONAL DUMB WEEK each year, to follow, say, BE KIND TO ANIMALS WEEK held annually in the

United States. During this week, according to the rough plans I have drawn up, every man, woman and child would be compelled to keep silent for seven days and nights, under penalty of being locked up in a sound-proof detention pen. Absolute quietude would be compulsory for 168 hours. Talking would be prohibited even to one's self, or in one's sleep. There would be no theatrical performances permitted, no motion pictures, no radio, no lectures, no public gatherings. Just silence. And peace.

To make the plan more effective in an educational way, edicts would be issued warning humans to keep away from the members of their own species as much as possible, and to spend all available time with a dog. In other words, they would be ordered to "go to the dogs" as one should go to the dogs—to find sparkling companionship, and have one's heart stretched to larger proportions. By not talking for a week the human would be able to divert the flow of this usually wasted energy into more constructive channels and become of greater use to his community.

With his talking shut off, the human would automatically come to observe life in a more penetrating and discriminating way, not only physically, but mentally and spiritually. Then, with a dog to companion him and lead the way, he would be off on the road to more fascinating adventures than he ever dreamed existed. And sooner or later, if he kept on adventuring out towards the circumference of all things, he would make one of the greatest of all discoveries. This! That he was interrelated with everything in the universe, and that everything in the universe was capable of communicating with him . . . exchanging ideas with him . . . and giving him good counsel and direction. And if he were wise enough to let them help him, and to be his part of the Fellowship, he would eventually arrive at the place where he would be able to see the Creator moving through His full creation, and to hear the Creator speaking through His full creation. And what more could any of us ask than that?

*I'll be seeing you*

# STAGE WHISPERS

*New York*

*To*

*Strongheart*
*Eternal Playground*
*Out Yonder*

Dear old Pal:

For a dog that is supposed to be dead, buried, and through with existence for ever and ever, you certainly can be vitally effective at times in these areas that humans rope off as "the land of the living," and tonight was one of those occasions. As part of my New York visit I had dinner with two old and much-liked friends, one of them a theatrical producer and the other his business manager. Both are top men in their profession and, in spite of their hard-boiled attitudes about most things, delightful companions. Now under ordinary circumstances we would have joked and laughed our way through the hours we were together. But their minds were disturbed. Their latest play, which was produced less than three weeks ago, is threatening to do a financial nose-dive, and they don't know what to do about it.

So instead of our usual fun and frolic, they moaned and groaned about their play. Here is their problem: they insist they have a good play, that it is well cast, and that it has been produced with skill and charm. But not enough people are coming to see it to pay the bills. Why? Well, they did not seem to know, and I was prevented from tossing in opinions because of not having seen it. So they argued, and argued, and argued, while I sat there wondering how I might get their minds to spinning in orbits in which I could join them. Suddenly I heard something that set my mental ears straight up. There was friction in the company, ill feeling among the players because of professional jealousies. But my friends were so accustomed to such things that they paid no attention to them.

At their next conversational pause, I told them that any dog running the streets of New York could show them what was wrong with their play And not only that, but that any dog running the streets of New York could teach their high-salaried cast how to turn it into a success. Well, sir, I wish you could have seen their faces. For once in their lives they were inarticulate. They did not know whether I was trying to insult them, or be funny. And they were in no mood for either. Before they could start their tongues wagging again, I asked if either of them had ever heard of a dog being a failure as an actor in the theater or in motion pictures.

They stared at me like two puzzled children, and then shook their heads. They had never known of a dog giving an unsuccessful performance. I asked them how they accounted for such an amazing fact in the world of entertainment. The business manager didn't even try, beyond observing that it was "just one of those things that nobody could explain." The producer ventured the opinion that it was probably because dogs were called upon to be only themselves in plays, plus the fact that people "naturally liked dogs." He assumed a very judicial air. Then he said, "It is something we have inherited." That was the complete answer.

I asked them how many amateur and professional human actors "flopped" every year in the United States; that is, failed to give either satisfying or successful performances when they had the opportunity? Their guesses ran into incredible thousands. When they had finished I said to them, "If there is no record of a dog actor being unsuccessful in public performance, and so many human actors are constantly failing in their efforts, wouldn't it be a wise managerial thing to find out just what it is the dogs have which makes them so universally successful and popular, and inject some of it into the humans?"

Then I brought you into the situation. The mere mention of your name animated their faces. They knew more about you than I would have believed. They had seen all of your pictures not once but many times, and had the most profound respect for you as a dog and as a dramatic actor. But what do you think impressed them most about you? Your ability to pile up such big box-office grosses. That was like sweet music in their ears. They always talk impressively about their interest in the art of the theater, and even in the art of motion pictures, but their interest usually lasts only as long as the art pays dividends. So your money-earning capacities gave you exceptionally high honor with them.

When they learned how well you and I knew one another they were eager to know the "inside secrets" about you, just what it was that made you such a success. I told them that as far as I had been able to observe there were no secrets about you at all. Your director, I pointed out, had simply helped you to rise above many of the limitations which humans so thoughtlessly clamp down on dogs. And that having risen above them, you acted accordingly, much to the astonishment and delight of audiences everywhere. That intrigued them. They wanted to know more about you. They were beginning to get their mental fingers on something new and professionally interesting to them.

"I will share with you something I found out about him that revolutionized my thinking about a lot of things," I told them. "Something that ought to be helpful for every human that appears in front of audiences. Let me begin by saying that one of the things in the Strongheart pictures that puzzled and baffled me was the acting of some of my friends. Ordinarily these actors were capable 'troupers' either in stage or screen plays, but whenever they appeared with Strongheart there was a decided slump in their work. At first I thought it might be due to pride, that deep within themselves they were professionally ashamed of having to play subordinate roles to a dog in an ' animal opera.' But when they assured me that they liked acting with the dog, I knew I would have to dig deeper.

"One day I made what to me was an extraordinary discovery. Those actor friends were doing the best they could with the roles they were portraying, but their best was not good enough to keep up with the pace being set by the dog. Strongheart was not only outperforming them, he was making them look amateurish. He was running away with every scene he appeared in, and there was nothing they could do to prevent it. The moment the dog appeared, audiences lost interest in the humans. He rose above and dominated the story, the members of the cast, the production, and even the scenery.

"Watching him from behind a continuous question mark, I gradually began discovering his 'success formula'; and the more I found out about it, the more I began to understand why he had such universal audience appeal. What counted most in this 'formula' was not his outward appearance, impressive as that was. Nor his unusual intelligence and the remarkable things he was able to do with it, although these were contributing factors. It was his character. His integrity. His attitude towards life. The fine things he stood for inwardly and outwardly.

"I hunted through a dictionary and made a list of every good quality I had ever seen percolate through him in public and private life, noting particularly how he used them. It was a revelation. The list ran into many, many hundreds; and remember, every one of them was a quality of the highest excellence. I did the same thing with my human actor friends. Then I compared the lists. The reason for the dog's superior drawing power on the stage and in motion pictures was as plain as day. He was making better use, more consistent use, of his qualities in both public and private life. The humans had the advantage over him in such things as intellectual education, technical training, experience, the speech arts, and the use of make-up and costumes. But the dog was outshining them from the inside! And that inner radiation 'packed 'em in' wherever he appeared, or his pictures were shown.

"The humans and the dog were using different methods in their stage and screen work, and getting different results. The humans were in the habit of giving of themselves in varying degrees, depending to a great extent on the play, the part they were doing, their opinion of director and cast, and the state of their feelings and emotions. True, they were sincerely interested in the mental and physical efforts they were putting into their parts, but with it they were mixing an even greater interest, an interest having to do entirely with themselves; an interest concerned with what their particular part would do for them in the way of self-satisfaction, applause, reputation, money, press notices, fame and career. 'Kingdoms divided against themselves,' so to speak.

"Strongheart, on the other hand, was perfectly coördinated within and without. He had no divided interests. No objective ambitions. No jealousies. No envy. No pettiness. No temperament. No ill will. No ego urges. No pretense. His main purpose was to get all of himself into outward circulation. To move constantly from the center of himself to his circumference. He was always looking for opportunities to share himself. When he found them he let go with everything he had. Like all dogs, he never gave less than his best, never gave less than his all. I never knew him to cheat in matters of this kind. He always made full use of his capacities. He put on just as fine a show playing with an old shoe in a back yard with no one looking on, as he did when doing dramatic feats in front of wildly enthusiastic audiences. He was always as much of his complete selfhood as he knew how to be. And remember he was supposed to be 'only a dog.'

"His inner goodness and its outer expression were so genuine and so appealing that men, women, and children of every nation, starved for the things he was diffusing so generously, turned to him as naturally and as instinctively as flowers turn to the light. They couldn't help it. He had what they wanted, what they needed. I doubt if anyone ever turned away from him unsatisfied, or unnourished. People thought they were watching an unusually well-trained dog doing unusual things. What they were really doing, though, was looking through a moving transparency on four legs, and seeing a much better universe than the one they had been living in. That is why they were always so eager to come back for more looks. And, that, incidentally, explains those box-office records."

Then we said goodbye and went our various ways.

*I'll be seein' you*

# NUDISTS

*To*

*Strongheart*
*Eternal Playground*
*Out Yonder*

Dear old Pal :

That the substance, the power, and the influence of a life well-lived are as illimitable as they
are deathless, even though that life be "only a
dog's," has again been demonstrated. And with
you, my dear Strongheart, as the hub of the
verification. It came as an aftermath of the dinner
discussion I had with those two theatrical friends
of mine, which I told you about in my last letter.
When we said goodbye that night, I did not expect
to see them again for a long time, but early the
next morning they were at my hotel. And what
do you suppose they wanted ? More talk about
you, especially that humanly unseen, inner part
of you which enabled you to look and function as
you did.

What arrested their interest the night we talked
was my telling them that your popularity and
success as an actor had been due more to your
withinness than to your withoutness, to your
sterling qualities of character, more than to your
physical appearance or your ability to perform as
you did. Now I am well enough acquainted with

PI                            217

them to know that if I had said in ordinary conversation that fine inner qualities were absolutely essential for fine acting, they would have run me mentally footsore with their contrary arguments and wisecracks. But having you to back me up put an entirely different light on the matter. In the first place, they have the deepest respect for your achievements. And in the second, as practical showmen they were eager to find out at firsthand just how you became such a "gold mine" in the desert lands of entertainment. They had probably been figuring that if a dog could do as well as you did with certain inner qualities, a human equipped with them would be able to accomplish almost anything.

Up to the time I took you apart for them so that they could see how you "ticked," they had never seriously regarded "luminous withinness" as essential in an actor. They had been accustomed to working with externals. They were not particularly interested in an actor's state of mind, but in his looks, his wardrobe, his speech, and his ability to play the role given him. As we talked the next morning, with you as a kind of glorified pivot, we came to the ever-interesting question of why it is that children and dogs have such universal appeal, whether met across footlights, on a motion-picture screen, or in private life. That meant going back of physical appearances and actions, and into the realm of the mental and the emotional.

Looking for these causes set us to hunting for qualities—childlike and doglike qualities;— at least they did the hunting while I wrote down their findings. It was a new game for those two "hard-boiled theatrical eggs," and they played it with zest and relish. When they were through I read their lists back to them. Without their being conscious of it, every quality with "attraction values" they had mentioned had to do with uprightness of character and conduct. There isn't room to set down all the qualities they found, but here are enough to give you the general flavor : goodness . . . singleness of purpose . . . animation . . . enthusiasm . . . wholesomeness . . . happiness . . . naturalness . . . simplicity . . . friendliness . . . guilelessness . . . universality of outlook . . . high spirits . . . teachableness . . . purity . . . adaptability . . . spontaneity . . . modesty . . . unselfishness . . . sincerity . . . honesty . . . freedom from self-consciousness . . . large-heartedness . . . and free giving.

As they examined and re-examined these gracious assets of children and dogs, not as philosophical speculators but as seasoned showmen interested only in "hard facts and figures," the producer arrived at what to him was a new and exciting conclusion. Let me break it up into its five component parts. One : that it is in the natural order of things for people to be drawn towards that which is genuinely good, regardless of its form, classification, or method of expression. Two: that most children and dogs have this genuine goodness to the depths of their being. Three: that this goodness usually radiates through them like light through a transparency. Four: that people will always pay money to watch it.

Five: and so children and dogs, with few exceptions, cannot help being good box-office.

Then, by way of contrast, we talked about the unchildlike and undoglike qualities that the average sophisticated, self-interested, self-promoting human carries around with him in his mind and heart, and breathes into everything he says and does. Again they played their game, only this time they piled up negative and unlovely qualities. They certainly had no illusions about the human in his unspiritualized state. I shall not set down their findings, they were too unpleasant. Suddenly without the slightest warning the producer bounded out of his chair exclaiming: "I've got it! I know what's wrong with the play!" Then he shook hands, told me he would see me later, grabbed his hat and coat, and hurried away, with his business manager almost on his heels.

The idea which catapulted him out of his chair, I learned later, was, briefly, this: "If the inner perfection of children and dogs has such a powerful and irresistible audience pull, then any inward imperfections in matured humans would naturally have an opposite, or repelling effect with audiences." The producer called his company together in his office, locked the doors, and, with you as a glittering example of what "even a dog" was able to accomplish with the right kind of inner and outer coördination, held what was probably the most unique conference in Broadway history.

The producer told me afterwards that it was one of the most revolutionizing experiences he had ever been through. Everyone seemed to have turned himself inside out for mental inspection and to have enjoyed the experience. None of the players had ever given more than casual interest to the quality of their thinking, or to its probable effect on others. They had been under the impression that what went on in their own thought areas was strictly their own business; that as long as their outer appearance and performance were satisfactory, they had fulfilled their obligations to both employer and audience. They had neglected to take into consideration that thoughts are motor; and that thinking, by inevitable law, always externalizes and proclaims itself in some way, whether one desires it or not.

Those actors and actresses had been walking around mentally naked in front of audiences without being aware of it. They did not know that they, like all the rest of us, were mental nudists in a transparent universe! A nudists' universe, in which nothing whatsoever could be hidden or concealed. They had not expanded enough to understand that those skin-and-bone bodies of theirs, which they spent so much time feeding, grooming, decorating, clothing, indulging, worrying about and idolizing, were, scientifically speaking, only shadow-stuff. Cellophane wrappers, so to speak, through which anyone with discernment might look whenever he pleased and see what was going on within!

Fortunately the members of the cast were not afraid of new ideas. Or of flashlighting their own minds and hearts. Added to this they were intelligent, they had imagination and humor, and a sincere desire to save their play from the financial rocks. So, "naked and unashamed," they talked things through. At the right moment the producer told them that while they had been doing a satisfactory job with their outward performances, they had been consistently wrecking the show with their mental attitudes; pointing out to them that their discordant thinking was not only permeating everything they were saying and doing on the stage, but was seeping across the footlights like escaping gas and affecting people in the theater, and even potential audiences outside the theater. "For who," he asked in a question worth framing and hanging on the wall, "can estimate the bounds and influence of thinking which is capable of being stretched out to include planets millions of light-years away?"

Their conclusions about audiences are worth repeating. Previous to the meeting most of them had regarded the average audience as just so many people out front looking for entertainment, which they, the performers, were providing by acting make-believe stories. But after pooling their experiences and observations, with your inner and outer record thrown in for good measure, and after giving the matter earnest consideration, they decided that audiences were individual, living and breathing "radio sets," that were sensitive and responsive not only to the sight and sound vibrations coming across the footlights, but, in varying degrees of receptivity, to the thought qualities and purposes set in vibration by author, producer, director and players.

With this to round out their series of discoveries the producer staged his climax. He asked how many of them would join him in an honest effort to live up to dog standards for the balance of the run of the play; that is, to be at one's best, to live one's best, and to give only one's best—come what may. All agreed. That night they gave a truly inspired performance. Better by far, I am told, than on opening night. It was an individually coördinated performance, a unified performance, and so a great performance. But even more important than the acting, the mental currents going across the footlights had a tang to them which stimulated and refreshed. Since then the play has been zooming up to the altitudes where it belonged in the first place. Its success is now assured. Once again dog technique is paying dividends.

*I'll be seein' you*

# WINDOWS

*To*

*Strongheart*
*Eternal Playground*
*Out Yonder*

Dear old Pal:

I am rolling Westward towards California. This is the same railroad that once upon a time carted you to Hollywood in a baggage car as just another dog; and within two years triumphantly transported you Eastward as an internationally famous motion-picture star, attended by a manager, a valet and a press representative. Remember all the crowds that waited for you at ever train stop? And the official gentlemen who patted your head, extended to you the freedom of their cities, and were photographed with you? You certainly were a good illustration of a small-town dog making good in a big way. I mention these things merely as a coincidence, as I know how much you disliked crowds of humans and their emotional adulation.

Since early morning I have been sitting here in a luxurious chair looking through a broad window and watching the United States hurry by as though late for an appointment on the Atlantic seaboard. Like you, I am a window addict. I never seem to find enough windows to look through. All kinds give me pleasure, except perhaps those that look out on blank walls or have bars in them. My favorites are skylights and portholes. If it were possible, I would carry a private window-frame around with me, just to look through at views I particularly like. I consider myself rather good as a window looker-outer, but I have to admit that my best has never equaled your average. Watching you survey life through a window was not only an inspiration, but an education.

I wish I knew more about dogs' inner and outer vision, and what they really "take in" when they stare through house and automobile windows with such keen interest. We humans have to admit that you dogs are capable of "picking up" physical objects far beyond the range of our human eyesight. But dog perception is far greater than that, I know. You taught me so. Many and many a time when we were together, you "saw" and identified people coming to visit us long before you could get their scent or hear them; and some time before they came close enough physically for me to know about it. It always irked me that I, with my supposedly superior faculties, could not discern them when you did. You showed me, too, that nearly all dogs have the capacity to see beyond physical forms and read things not apparent to material eyes; but how far this field of observation extends I do not know. It would be interesting, perhaps even revolutionizing, to know how the dog's inner perception and the human's inner vision are related. We humans believe that the highest accomplishment with vision is the ability to see God in everything.

But to get back to windows. There is an almost unbridgeable difference between the attitude of the average human towards windows and that of the window-addict. The former may appreciate windows but is usually more or less indifferent to them, except as they let in or shut out light, air, sunshine and sound. To the addict every window is endowed with charm and sorcery. He regards them as magic casements placed where they are for but one purpose: to afford him an opportunity to escape mentally and spiritually for the kind of adventures he knows to be more exciting and satisfying than any of the close-to-earth kind. Adventures in which he does not have to drag his skin-and-bone body after him. Adventures limited only by the bounds of his imagination.

The country we have been going through this afternoon is as fine as there is between the Atlantic and Pacific Oceans. It is what I always think of as your kind of country—spacious, rugged, unspoiled by the hand of man—and everything is saturated with sunshine, crispness and fragrance. A short while ago we circled some foothills and came upon a panorama of loveliness that made me gasp! The foreground was a vast patchwork quilt of ranches, towns, forest, lakes and rivers; the background, range after range of towering snow-capped mountains extending as far as the eyes could see. And every inch of it reflecting rainbow colors from a low-slanting sun. It was pure grandeur!

In the presence of such divine wonder-work,

226

every human aboard the train should have been on his knees in humble, reverent appreciation, with his nose flattened against window-glass. I looked up and down our car to see what the other passengers were doing about it. Of the eleven men and women, four were playing cards, one was writing, two were reading, one had his eyes opened but appeared to be in a state of suspended animation, and the rest were asleep. Such indifference demanded further investigation. I walked the length of the train. Only three people were watching that glorious color pageant outside, and one of these was yawning. The rest were engaged in what my species calls "killing time." Their windows might just as well have been boarded up.

That is one travel fact. But here is another. Up ahead in one of the baggage cars are five delightful dogs on their way to Los Angeles. They, too, are passengers, but are riding like prisoners. They have no space to move around in, no one to share themselves with, no windows to look through and see where they are going. All they can do is to stand, sit or lie; and wonder what it's all about, and why it had to happen to them. In all fairness this whole train situation should be reversed, and the humans placed in the baggage cars, and the dogs brought back here and given an opportunity to make use of these humanly unappreciated windows. The dogs would be grateful for it; and the humans could carry on their reading, writing, card-playing, dozing, day-dreaming, gossiping, and thinking about themselves just as well in the windowless baggage cars as they are doing in their present places. Perhaps even better.

As far as railroad regulations are concerned, the dogs are being treated well enough. But they deserve more freedom and more companionship. They really should be riding on top of the train behind a wind-break, where they could survey full horizons, and sniff the latest news from the passing air currents. I met all five dogs socially the first time the train stopped long enough for them to be taken out and exercised. Since then we have become great friends. Every time I stick my head into their temporary jail they almost pull the place apart in their excitement. They all seem to be shouting at once, "Come on, fellow, get us out of here! Life's too precious to be wasted in a place like this. Let's go out and stir up some fun! You spring us loose, and we'll show you how!" If I had a few less inhibitions I would do it, too. I would like nothing better than to liberate them, and make a break for the hills with or rather after them. We would be chased and caught, of course. And they would be locked up, and so would I, but without their engaging company. But even at that it might be worth it.

I wish they would let me bring back one of those dogs in the baggage car, and introduce him to the man across the aisle from me. If ever a man needed a dog, he does. I don't know who he is, but he seems to be important and prosperous. He has been having a miserable time, and apparently enjoying it, ever since we left New York. He has been irritable, bad-tempered and bad-mannered all the way. Nothing inside or outside the train pleases him. I think I know what is wrong with him. He has been milling around too much with the human species, and the experience has soured him, and thrown him out of gear with life. His outgo, upgo, and ongo have been shut off.

His acidity of mind, heart, body and experience is by no means an uncommon malady; as a matter of fact, it is quite prevalent among my kind. Its cure by human methods is often slow and difficult, but under dog treatment the victims usually recover quickly and permanently. Any one of those dogs in the baggage car could take my crabbed, caustic neighbor out of the devitalizing state he is in, and set him to moving in harmony and rhythm with the Cosmos again. What he seems to need more than anything else is to have his interests and affections turned outward, turned away from himself. And that, preeminently, is a dog's job. It wouldn't be possible for my coagulated friend across the way to be with one of those dogs and at the same time think about himself. They are much too entertaining, too amusing, too affectionate, too sympathetic, too appreciative, too supercharged with life, too filled with good things to share.

I know how they would go to work on him. They would first open his eyes so that he could see what a delightful world he is in. Then they would open his heart, his mind, and his whole being to be grateful for it. Then they would induce him to play with them. And that would start the real cure; for if a human, or a dog, or any other kind of animal is able to play, he can be taught. And if he is teachable, he is capable of unlimited development and accomplishment. That was one of the great "secrets" about your success. Larry Trimble, your instructor, was unable to do much of anything with you as a highly trained, regimented, military and police dog. Your outlook on life was too narrow and savage. But after he showed you how to play, you became so teachable that he was able to help you develop to the remarkable degree you did. If it worked so well on you, it certainly ought to do something for my neighbor across the aisle.

*I'll be seein' you*

# WOLVES

*To*
*Strongheart*
*Eternal Playground*
*Out Yonder*

Dear old Pal:

Speaking as one who has seen much of the motion-picture industry in an intimate way, let me say that if a vote were taken for the most outstanding movie enchantress of all time, I would unhesitatingly write on my ballot *Lady Silver*. And were I given to wagering, I would be willing to lay fairish odds that no one will top her for a long time to come. I say this not because she was your most successful leading lady, and one of your favorite playmates, but solely because of her merits as an actress. True, she was only a wolf, but she was good enough at being only a wolf to win screen and advertising credits above all the humans in her pictures; to win an international name for herself; and to force even you to divide audience interest with her.

It is not surprising that I should be thinking about her today as the train is passing through Colorado; for in the distance I can see the mountains where once upon a time she used to run free and wide, until her foot was caught in a trap. Zoölogists classified her as an unusually fine specimen of timber wolf, silver-gray in color, eighty-five pounds in weight, and approximately two years old. But like you and all other forms of life that have the courage to be themselves, Lady Silver was beyond such things as classifications and definitions.

What a fascinating creature she was with her sleek, powerful, lithesome body; her restless energy; and her swift, rhythmical way of doing things! She was shy, gentle, affectionate and playful when she believed in you and trusted you. But what a mess of trouble she could be when annoyed. How she could fling herself into action with those strong, wide-gaping jaws of hers, and those sharp, deep-hacking fangs! There was never any quibbling with her, was there! When trouble moved into her vicinity she always struck first, and usually without any preliminary warning. And how she could fight! I don't suppose anything on four legs ever got the best of her.

Lady Silver played or fought with equal facility. She made every living thing that came near her respect her. And when, by a peculiar series of circumstances, she got her chance in the movies, she made everyone inside and outside the film industry respect her, too. She had "what it takes," didn't she? Apparently nothing on two or four legs could resist her. Bless her! I wonder where she is now! Out there in the Eternal Playground with you? Running free in the mountains here in the West? Looking out from a cage in some zoo or circus? Well, wherever she is, that place is much the better for her being there.

And where do you suppose all the other members of her famous pack are at the present time? I don't remember all their names, but there was Flash, and Lobos, and Mike, and Ike, and Sibe, and Red Dog, and Gay Girl, and Inyo, and Mono, and Trixie, and that comical, rough playing Tommy with his one hundred and twenty-five pounds of almost ceaseless motion. I doubt if anything in motion pictures ever created a greater sensation than those wolves. Up until their film debut, few humans had ever seen a real wolf pack in action. Hence the sensation. How humans, wolves and sledge-dogs could be photographed in such an intimately realistic way was, and still is, a mystery to most people. That a single wolf could be trained to perform in front of motion-picture cameras was not too much of a strain on human imagination. But to persuade an entire pack to do so became something resembling sorcery. For after all, camera lines are camera lines, and wolves are wolves.

It baffled me, too, until I tip-toed behind the scenes and unearthed the secret. You know about it from your angle, of course, but let me tell it to you from mine. Two of the dramatic North Woods stories you starred in called for a pack of "ferocious, man-eating wolves." There were a few wolves available for picture work in the country, but no packs of them. Movie makers are ingenious, though, and especially was this true of your director, Larry Trimble. To get his pack he did a simple, typically American thing. He advertised for wolves in newspapers published in wolf country, asking that available wolves be sent to him in care of a concentration camp in Colorado.

The response was immediate. Wolves were sent to him from zoos, trappers, ranchers, hunters, trading posts and plain, ordinary citizens. Out of this wild and crazy assortment Trimble selected twenty-three of the biggest, healthiest, and strongest and shipped them to Canada where a special stockade covering many acres had been built for them. Into this the wolves were dumped. Fighting began at once and went on intermittently day and night, especially at night, when the wolf is supposed to be at its best. Out of that battling assortment a victor and leader had to emerge. Eventually one did. It was Lady Silver. The others were good in their wolfing ways, but Lady Silver was better. Immeasurably so! She had all the requirements for pack leadership: sex appeal . . . intelligence . . . cunning . . . keen perception . . . discrimination . . . strength . . . speed . . . agility . . . endurance . . . courage . . . fearlessness . . . integrity in the moral code of the wolf . . . and unusual fighting ability. In her conquest of the pack, Lady Silver first fought the other females to a standstill, and then, with an artful mixture of blandishments and fangs, put the males in their proper places. After that, she ruled supreme.

Then Larry Trimble did one of the "eccentric" things for which he is noted. He moved into the stockade and began living in there with the wolves, doing his writing there, eating his meals there, and at night sleeping in a hole in the snow the way the wolves did, except that he made use of an Arctic bedroll. In one way it was a foolhardy thing to do, as he went in there unarmed and had no way of protecting himself in case of attack. But Trimble had this advantage: he understood the workings of a wolf's mind and heart. He knew from long experience with them that the wolf, instead of being the bad character depicted in so many stories, is really a fine fellow when one gets to know him; that the wolf has all the excellent qualities, and even more, possessed by the domestic dog; that it has a genuine desire to be with and coöperate with humans; and that its unfriendly behavior at times in its wild state is simply its defense reactions to the cruelty, ruthlessness and pitilessness of man.

That is why he carried no weapons into the stockade with him. He was aware that the wolves would read his mental attitudes the moment he stepped inside, and that going armed either physically or mentally would create resistance and antagonism, and defeat his plans right at the start. Trimble knew that his only success lay along the delicate line of breaking down the barriers of suspicion, fear and enmity existing between the wolves and himself; and then winning their complete confidence, respect and friendship.

For many weeks Trimble lived in the stockade. During most of this time the wolves kept as far away from him as possible, but near enough to keep him under continuous observation. Outside of throwing food to them, Trimble made no gestures in their direction. He wanted them to

235

get to know him in their own way. Gradually their fear and suspicion of him turned into wonder. Then the wonder turned into curiosity. Then the curiosity turned into interest. Then the interest turned into a timid desire to know the man better. One afternoon Lady Silver came cautiously up to where Trimble was preparing their evening meal and accepted food from his hand. The next day she came accompanied by four other wolves. On the third day the whole pack came in close and dined with him. The barriers were down. That night the wolves dug their sleeping holes near to where Trimble slept.

As the months rolled along, the understanding between Trimble and the wolves expanded to such a degree that they followed him around the open countryside like domestic dogs. But what was more important, they followed him back into the stockade again after every jaunt. With tactful handling the dogs and the humans were introduced to the wolves and taught to play together. Then they were ready to make pictures. For the superdramatic scenes of wolves trailing down humans to kill them, Trimble simply maneuvered his four-legged friends across camera lines. To the audience it was breath-taking suspense; but to the wolves it was only playing follow-the-leader with Trimble in the lead. And those blood-curdling fight scenes between wolves, dogs and humans! Nothing more than a happy family of animals and humans playing rough-and-tumble and enjoying it hugely. Although when photographed, it looked as though they were tearing one another apart.

Trimble used the same basic method in educating the wolves that he has with all the other wild and domestic animals he has worked with. He kept them well fed, happy, playful and contented. He taught them always to turn to him as their friend when perplexed or afraid. He lifted all mental limitations off them. He made their schooling such fun that they were eager to learn, to expand, and to coöperate with him. Thus they came to respect him, to respect themselves, and to respect what they were doing. The wolves were never forced, never threatened, never punished, and never even scolded when they made mistakes. Kindness, consideration, patience, wise discipline, encouragement, affection and appreciation were the invariable rule.

Out of this blossomed the never-to-be-forgotten wolf pack. Their success, Lady Silver's success, and your success are now motion-picture history. Those pictures were an outstanding contribution to world entertainment. But even more important, I believe, was the neat way in which Larry Trimble, with his quiet voice and gentle touch, debunked the wolf of its evil reputation; and demonstrated with a whole pack of them fresh from the wilds how desirous wolves are for friendly and loyal coöperation with man, whenever man is willing to do his part.

*I'll be seein' you*

# JOURNEY'S END

*Hollywood*
*California*

*To*

*Strongheart*
*Eternal Playground*
*Out Yonder*

Dear old Pal:

This letter marks journey's end. Less than an hour ago my baggage and I were deposited on the front steps of our little house, and that ceremony formally completed the girdling of the globe. From now on everything that happens belongs to another adventure. At the moment I am sitting in that old Mexican chair, feet on balcony rail, writing-pad in my lap, basking in the sun. It is a winter day but like midsummer. I haven't unpacked a thing. I am waiting for a little girl who lives up the street to come down and boss the job. I promised her I would. She is very young, as years are counted, but has the airs of a grandmother. She is my favorite audience. Almost everything that happens interests and delights her. She is like a dog in her genuineness, unselfed outlook, radiant joy, enthusiasms and gratitude for the privilege of living. That is why I want her here for the unpacking.

It is going to take a long time to assort and assimilate the impressions gathered since last I sat

238

on this porch. At the moment, the trip seems like a fantastic dream. I suppose that comes from having been on the move almost continuously by land and sea and air, visiting so many countries, and doing so many unusual things. During these wanderings I had an opportunity to fraternize and exchange ideas with representatives of all sorts of national, religious, philosophical and social systems. That was a broadening and deepening experience. But what was even more interesting and instructive was the opportunity to do the same thing with a wide assortment of wild and domestic animals, birds, insects, snakes, and other quite remarkable fellows listed by my species as "lower forms of life."

The latter part of that paragraph would certainly require much explaining if this letter were being written to a human. It might even involve me in having to sit in the midst of a group of white-coated, serious-faced gentlemen for a sanity test. But the animals, and the birds, and the insects, and the snakes seemed to understand. So will you. And so, I believe, will all those adventurous individuals who have ever explored above the low mental ceilings, and out beyond the restricted mental frontiers of the human species.

Considering all the opportunities the human has had for observation, research, study and experiment, it seems unbelievable that he should be so backward in discovering and identifying himself with the worlds of enriching relationships lying all about him outside of his own kind. I suppose there are innumerable reasons for this. The iconoclasts among us say that it comes from organized ignorance; that, boiled down to bare facts, most of us are so lacking in genuine intelligence as to be unable to grasp how highly intelligent the non-human part of creation really is. They insist we are not growing and expanding as we should because our excessive vanity and exclusiveness have made us so biologically bound, so species bound, and so self-bound that most of our natural outgo and ongo has been shut off.

If he thinks about it at all, the average human, with some degree of religious training, believes, at least in a nebulous sort of way, that all living creatures receive their life, being, energy, intelligence, capacities and abilities from the same infinitely divine Fountain-source. But with it he usually blends the conviction that this omnific Source, this great boundless, universal primal Intelligence which he has been taught to reverence as God, uses only the human species as the medium for His omniscient wisdom and His important purposes. Now how would you fellows outside the human species figure that one out?

The more advanced among my species do not subscribe to the above. They believe that because the God-intelligence and the God-power fill all space, and permeate all things, intelligence is everywhere present. So instead of giving ear only to those of their own species, they attune themselves inwardly, and listen for the great Voice of Existence which, they say, speaks continuously to receptive hearts, through all things, at all times, in all places.

It is reported that in the long ago when creation was like a big, happy family, language, except that which went from heart to heart silently and understandingly, was unnecessary, because everything was in such perfect and harmonious accord. That was a period when every living thing is said to have been completely loyal to its Cosmic obligations; when every living thing contributed itself utterly to the common good, and to the common happiness. Then something went wrong; and the human set out to walk apart from the rest of creation, to narrow his relationships, his sympathies, and his affections. From that time on, his troubles and sorrows began.

Apropos of all these things, let me repeat some rare, but as yet little understood, wisdom from one of humanity's most cherished books—the Bible. And I quote from the twelfth chapter of the Book of Job as translated by James Moffatt:

> *Ask the very beasts, and they will teach you;*
> *ask the wild birds—they will tell you;*
> *Crawling creatures will instruct you,*
> *the fish in the sea will inform you;*
> *For which of them all knows not*
> *that this is the Eternal's way,*
> *In whose control lies every living soul,*
> *and the whole life of man.*

For your information, the Book of Job is considered not only one of the finest masterpieces in world literature, but one of the greatest epics of the inner life of a human ever written. Symbolically Job is every man. His ride on the earth planet was an eventful one, to say the least.

Almost everything that can happen to a mortal happened to him. He managed to get to the peak of what most humans consider success, prosperity and importance; but he came down again with a crash which still echoes and re-echoes through the corridors of time. But let this be said of him: he did not stay "crashed." He got out of his difficulties, and the way he did it has been chart and compass for millions upon millions of humans ever since. But I wonder how many of them were able to grasp the far-reaching implications back of his advice about the beasts, and the birds, and the crawling creatures, and the fish? Or had imagination enough to try it?

Making use of some of the helpful postgraduate things you taught me, I made it a point on the journey around the world to talk mentally to everything that came within the range of my observation and interest—humans, animals, trees, flowers, oceans, winds, sun, moon, stars and so on. I tried always to speak from the heart, for that, experience has taught me, is the one language that every form of life understands and responds to. I tried to find in every living entity that golden thread of divinity which is supposed to hold all of us together in the animated tapestry of life. It was difficult to locate at times, especially in some of the human specimens. But when my patience was equal to the task, I was always able to find it; proving again and again how essentially good all life is, and how closely this inner goodness interrelates us to one another.

Keeping a friendly attitude towards everyone and everything was like carrying an invisible magic passport, which guaranteed me extra " safe and free passage" and extra "aid and protection" wherever I went. As a result I did not encounter one unfriendly human, animal, snake, or insect from the time I left until I returned a short time ago. Wherever I traveled with inward good will, tolerance, consideration, a desire to coöperate, understanding, gentleness and appreciation, those qualities came back to me in outward profusion from all directions—even from creeping and crawling things supposed to be deadly foes of man.

I would like to tell you more about this, but I must sign off, as that little girl is skipping down the street, attended by her small brother and two other lads. It looks like a picnic were in the making. This will be the last report for the present. I certainly had a marvelous time with the Universe on this long journey, and can only hope that the Universe had as good a time with me. If it did, the credit really belongs to you for showing me how to find, share, and enjoy rational relationships outside the confines of the human species. For this I shall always be your debtor. Thank you again, dear Strongheart, for being so completely—just *you.*

*I'll be seein' you*